Praise for (

"*Open Secrets* would make a good launching point for discussion among teachers of the most advanced spiritual disciplines of the world religions. He is a master teacher."
Father Thomas Keating

"The truth our hearts long for could not be more clearly or poignantly put than it is in this little book, *Open Secrets*, by Rami Shapiro. I will read this book again and again, reminded by it's clarity to remember what I thought I could never forget. Here is the essence of how the mystic within each of us sees reality, the truth that will take us home over and over again."
Oriah Mountain Dreamer, author of *The Invitation, The Dance,* and *The Call*

"These letters are diamonds. I shall re-read them often."
Andrew Harvey, author of *The Direct Path* and *The Passion of Rumi*

"*Open Secrets* is my favorite way to introduce readers to the essence and depth of Judaism. In such few words it goes right to the heart: "God is ALL!""
Bo Lozoff, author and founder of the Human Kindness Foundation

"In *Open Secrets*, Rabbi Rami Shapiro presents a universal wisdom with a distinctly Jewish flavor. This is a book to read and share."
Rodger Kamenetz, author of *The Jew in the Lotus*

"*Open Secrets* drew my heart closer to my roots. It opened the door for me to study the tradition of Judaism further. I highly recommend it as one of the best bridges of Eastern and Western wisdom."
Dennis Genpo Merzel, author of *The Path of the Human Being: Zen Teachings on the Bodhisattva Way*

"*Open Secrets* offers a rare spiritual journey into the heart of hasidic wisdom. Its beauty is in its simplicity and intimacy. I felt I was sitting in the presence of a great seer of India. Reb Yerachmiel's teachings echo ancient upanishadic truths, and reflect deep God-realization. The wisdom in these letters has the power to lift off the page and enter the heart. This book is written by a true man of God."
Sister Pravrajika Brahmaprana, Vedanta Convent

"These letters are vessels of teachings to enlighten and bring light to the spirit. Rami has an ecumenical, universal outlook in his philosophy that is most refreshing."
Swami Murugananda

OPEN SECRETS

Also by Rami M. Shapiro

Hasidic Tales: Annotated & Explained

Proverbs: The Wisdom of Solomon

The Way of Solomon: Finding Joy and Contentment in the Wisdom of Ecclesiastes

Minyan: Ten Principles for Living a Life of Integrity

Wisdom of the Jewish Sages: A Modern Reading of Pirke Avot

OPEN
SECRETS

The Letters of
Reb Yerachmiel ben Yisrael

RAMI M. SHAPIRO

MONKFISH BOOK PUBLISHING COMPANY
RHINEBECK, NEW YORK

Library of Congress Cataloging-in-Publication Data

Shapiro, Rami M.
  Open secrets : the letters of Reb Yerachmiel ben Yisrael / Rami M. Shapiro.
    p. cm.
  ISBN 0-9749359-2-1
  1. Judaism. 2. Jewish way of life. 3. Spiritual life--Judaism. 4. Imaginary
letters. I. Title.
  BM45.S462 2004
  296.7--dc22
                        2004012995

Book and cover design by Georgia Dent

Bulk purchase discounts for educational or promotional purposes are
available. Contact the publisher for more information.

First edition

First impression

10 9 8 7 6 5 4 3 2 1

Monkfish Book Publishing Company
27 Lamoree Road
Rhinebeck, New York 12572
www.monkfishpublishing.com

To Father Thomas Keating
whose unflagging love for Reb Yerachmiel and his teachings
kept the promise of this book alive.

ACKNOWLEDGMENTS

THIS BOOK HAS had a life of its own. Originally created as a handout for a seminar I offered at my Miami synagogue in the early nineties, these letters have been circulated in a variety of ersatz editions throughout North and South America. In 1994, *Open Secrets* found a home with Bo and Sita Lozoff and the Human Kindness Foundation. There it lived for ten years, as part of the mailings they send to residents of our nation's many prisons. I am grateful to Bo and Sita, and also to the hundreds of prisoners who have written me in appreciation of this book and its teachings.

The muse behind these letters is the real Aaron Hershel—my son. I wrote these letters shortly after his Bar Mitzvah. They were a distillation of my philosophy that I hoped to share with him during his adolescence. I don't know how well I did in that regard. For all my desire to impart these teachings to him, I also felt the need to allow him to discover them on his own. Maybe the book was my way of saying, "Here is the dad I meant to be. Here are the things I wanted to share with you." I am proud of my son and the man he has grown up to be. While most of the credit goes to his mother, Debbie, I will reserve a bit for Reb Yerachmiel and myself.

A few additional thank yous are vital here. First, to my rebbe Reb Zalman Schachter-Shalomi, whose concern for me and respect for my work led to the revival of this book. Second, to my friend and teacher Father Thomas Keating, whose endless enthusiasm for this book pushed me to find a commercial outlet for it. Third, to my publisher Paul Cohen of Monkfish whose willingness to back this venture turned Fr. Thomas's urgings into reality. And fourth, to my editor, Toinette Lippe. This is my fourth book with Toinette, and in some ways it has been the most satisfying. She has been involved with *Open Secrets* almost as long as I have: reading and rereading it, making suggestions to clarify both the text and the teaching, and encouraging me to stick with it even when the only home we could find for it was my desk drawer. Her eagerness to bring this book to fruition is a gift for which I am eternally grateful.

CONTENTS

Acknowledgments   *ix*

Preface   *xiii*

Introduction   3

An Invitation   6

Judaism   9

Who Is a Jew?   14

God   18

Creation   21

Humanity   25

Evil   28

Human Nature   32

Torah   37

Mitzvot   43

Shabbat and the Holy Days   46

Israel   51

Intermarriage   54

Why Be Jewish?   56

Soul   59

Walking Inward   64

To Listen and to Love   67

Is It Working?   72

Religion   75

Are All Religions True?   80

Spirituality   84

Prayer   87

Dreams   91

Truth   95

Faith and Reason   97

Be Holy   102

Jesus   106

Finding a Teacher   110

Death   113

Glossary   *117*

PREFACE

SEVERAL YEARS AGO I suddenly found myself without moorings. I was at the top of my profession: My congregation was thriving, my books were finding appreciative audiences, and I was invited to share my insights with my peers and their communities across the country. Yet something was terribly wrong. I felt stale and listless.

I talked with my family, my friends, my therapist, and while all were helpful in their way, none could taste the deep sense of loss that I was feeling, and thus none of them could speak what I needed to hear. So I turned to my rebbe.

I am not one to run to gurus. I have met many during my years as a student of religion, and even more in my over twenty years as a congregational rabbi. Some were charlatans, others genuine. Some were actually saints. I have stayed in contact with several of them, and have lived among their disciples and devotees. But I seem to lack the personality to be a real disciple, let alone a devotee. I am too opinionated, too sure of myself, and my need to lead makes it hard for me to follow. Yet I do have a rebbe, a rabbi whose sense of God's presence is far superior to my own.

There is a hasidic saying that goes something like this: There are two kinds of rebbes who experience the cold of winter. One buys a heavy coat, the other lights a fire. The first warms only himself, the second provides warmth for all who wish to draw near to his fire. My rebbe, Reb Zalman Schachter Shalomi, is a fire–lighter, and so I went to him for warmth, light, and direction.

I made arrangements to meet him during a weeklong retreat held at Elat Chayyim, the Jewish retreat center in Accord, New York. While we both had teaching obligations, there was plenty of time to speak together in private.

"Reb Zalman," I said, "I need some counsel. I have spoken with friends and therapists, and everyone is trying to help me discover what I want, but the truth is I do not know what I want. I have lost touch with my soul and can't discern the direction it wants me to go. I believe that you can see beyond my surface likes and dislikes, ambitions, and desires. I believe that you know my soul and can help me hear what advice it is giving. I need your help."

Reb Zalman was silent for quite a while. I was used to this. When asked to touch another's soul and speak on its behalf he was careful to put his ego aside, to silence his own voice so that the other could find the space to speak. After a while, however, it was clear to me that wherever Reb Zalman had gone he wasn't coming back any time soon. I was getting a little worried and not a little impatient.

"Reb Zalman?" I said softly, hoping to nudge him back into this world.

He blinked. He frowned. And then he looked at me and said "We'll speak about this later."

"Later" turned out to be almost a week later. Reb Zalman was walking with his wife Eve when he caught my eye and waved me over to him. The three of us found a shady spot where we could sit with some privacy. Reb Zalman looked into my eyes for a long moment and said:

"The other day you asked about what direction you should go in. I looked to see if I could discern your soul's path and did not like what I saw. Not at first, anyway. I had to be sure that what I was seeing was your soul and not some projection or distortion. We have been together a long time..."

"Almost twenty years." I said.

"... and I have followed your career closely. Your books, your courses, your teaching on the internet, all of it has had a profound impact on the Jewish people both here in America and around the world. You are, as I once wrote, a prophetic voice for a twenty-first-century Judaism. So when I saw what I saw I was not happy or sure I was seeing rightly. But every time I looked the seeing was always the same: enough with the Jews."

"Excuse me?" I said.

"Enough with the Jews," Reb Zalman repeated.

"I don't understand," I said.

"It is this way," he said. "You have completed your work among the Jewish people. Whatever you had to say to them has been said. The reason you are feeling lifeless is that you are repeating yourself. Your present world is an echo of your past. It is time to move on."

"Should I convert to Catholicism and become a priest?" I asked sarcastically.

"No. You are a Jew and a rabbi and this is right for you. But now you must take your philosophy beyond the walls of the synagogue."

"To proselytize? Am I supposed to become a missionary and convert people to Judaism?"

Reb Zalman sighed. "I knew you would not want to hear this," he said, "but this is what I think you need to do: shift your focus and bring your ideas to a wider audience. There is no need to convert anyone, but there is a need to enlighten people about what Judaism is and what it says. I am telling you to create a Judaism for non-Jews. I am suggesting that you offer a Judaism for people who wish to learn from it as they do from Buddhism or Sufism. I am telling you to create a Judaism for everyone, not just the Jews."

"And how am I going to do that?" I asked trying, and failing, to keep the fearful and angry edge out of my voice.

"Bring back Reb Yerachmiel."

Now it was my turn to fall silent. I had no idea that Reb Zalman was familiar with my connection to this nineteenth-century hasidic master. "Reb Yerachmiel is fiction," I said hoarsely.

Reb Zalman cupped my face in his strong dry hands. He kissed me and whispered close to my ear: "Reb Yerachmiel is not fiction. Reb Yerachmiel is you."

"I created him," I replied, "but...."

"But nothing. He is your alter ego. He is the rebbe you aspire to be. If you are not yet ready to embody him yourself, at least give him a voice. People respond to him and his teachings. If the only way for you to access this part of yourself is through Reb Yerachmiel, then do so."

"You want me to channel this fictional sage?"

"Yes. Let Reb Yerachmiel speak. His Judaism is what so many people hunger for."

On some level I knew Reb Zalman was right. I do tap the deepest part of me when I speak in Reb Yerachmiel's voice.

I decided to follow his advice. The book you hold in your hands is the result.

Open Secrets is written as a series of letters to my great–grandfather from Reb Yerachmiel ben Yisrael. I imagined them.

The Judaism of Reb Yerachmiel is the Judaism I have taught for over twenty years. It is the Judaism I practice and the Judaism I have passed on to my son and my students. I ask you to enter into the spirit of these letters, to allow yourself the freedom to engage the teachings of this twenty-first-century rebbe. The truth they contain does not rely on Reb Yerachmiel's history but on the accuracy of his vision of God and creation. I hope you find them a constant and comforting companion.

Rami M. Shapiro
Yamim Noraim 5765
September/October 2004

The Letters of
Reb Yerachmiel ben Yisrael

INTRODUCTION

WHENEVER I AM asked to conjure up an image of the classic East European Jew in America I think instantly of my father's father, my Zayde. It was he who set me on the path of Yiddishkeit (Jewish living and learning). It was he who rooted me in the tradition that shapes the person I have become. And yet he intended none of this. As far back as I can recall he was simply an old man struggling to make sense of his life in the context of his faith and tradition.

Zayde dressed in black. Black pants, dark suspenders, white shirt with bow tie, black jacket. My most cogent image is of him seated on a hard wood bench built into a corner of his whitewashed apartment reading from a worn and cracked black leather notebook. The pages of the book were yellow and tattered. Pieces of brittle paper often flaked off as he turned pages. Zayde would carefully gather these up and stuff them into the book close to the binding. Along with these flakes a host of other paper scraps stuck out from the book at odd angles.

Zayde kept the book in his jacket pocket. I imagine it never left his side, and while he read it often, he shared it with no one. I had always assumed it was an old book of Psalms.

When Zayde died at the age of ninety-nine I was studying at Hebrew Union College in Jerusalem. I did not fly home to attend the funeral, and was not around when my father disposed of his father's things. The black notebook disappeared.

Two decades later, while rummaging through some family stuff in my parents' basement, I came across a shoebox filled with some of Zayde's things. In it was the black notebook. I recognized it instantly and was flooded with the images of Zayde poring over its tightly inked pages. I took it upstairs, sat in the living room by the bay window, and opened the book. It was not a book of Psalms.

Zayde's notebook contained a series of letters from his father's rebbe, Yerachmiel ben Yisrael. My great-grandfather, Aaron Hershel, had been a hasid of Reb Yerachmiel somewhere in Russia. I know very little about my family's history. I know nothing about Reb Yerachmiel, nor could I find him listed in any study of Hasidism. All I know of him is these letters and the many sayings of his that my great-grandfather had scribbled on bits of paper and stuffed into this book.

The letters are addressed to Aaron Hershel. Reb Yerachmiel appears to have been responding to questions my great-grandfather posed to him in writing. The issues raised are perennial: the nature of God, the purpose of Creation, the reason for evil, suffering, and death. But the answers!

Reb Yerachmiel was a thinker outside the boundaries of normative Judaism. His Judaism must have been exceedingly radical for its day, yet today it speaks powerfully to those of us seeking a new understanding of Torah for a postmodern time. It is because of this that I have taken the time to translate these letters into English and present them in book form.

I present Reb Yerachmiel's letters without notes or comment, and without my great-grandfather's initial queries that, sadly, were never preserved. My aim is to reproduce the letters in a manner that allows the reader to encounter them just as my Zayde did. While I admit that this is a contemporary translation, I believe I have remained faithful to the original. All I have added are "chapter and verse" to Reb Yerachmiel's biblical and talmudic references.

Zayde was forever reading and rereading these short letters from Reb Yerachmiel. I find myself doing the same. The more I read them, the more I find the gentle wisdom for which I and so many others hunger.

I ask that you read these letters at least twice. Once to become familiar with Reb Yerachmiel's style and vocabulary, and a second time to allow his wisdom to permeate your own efforts to make sense of what is often a spiritually confused and confusing world.

An Invitation

My dearest Aaron Hershel,

A letter arrives for me from the United States of America! You can imagine the excitement all over our village: Who does Yerachmiel ben Yisrael know in America? I myself could not imagine who would write me from such a place, and when I opened the letter and discovered it was from you—*g'valt!* What joy!

You were a good student, Hershele, not the best, but good. I am honored that you have chosen to continue your studies with me. It will be a challenge, not simply because of the distance, but because of the message. You ask difficult questions, and I prefer the simplest answers. The more words, the easier it is to avoid saying anything.

My teaching is not—how might I say this delicately—normative. While I believe with all my heart in God, Torah, and Israel, I do not understand these as my teachers and my peers would have me do. What I teach is not, God forbid, heresy, but neither is it mainstream.

My teaching is simple. I work hard to keep it that way. It is easy to fool a person who knows little with teachings that say much. I am not a complicated man, and do not wish to appear as one. I am simple and so my Judaism is simple. So simple, in fact, that it need not be taken on faith, but can be tested by anyone who wishes to know its validity.

My Judaism is not rich in halachic (legalistic) nuances. I admit to not being the greatest student of the Talmud and Codes. I admit to dreaming while my peers were cracking their heads on *Mishnah* and *Gemorah* (the two books of law and ethics that make up the Talmud, the code book of Jewish living). I learned enough to get by. Isn't that a horrible thing for a rabbi to say? I am not even average, but a bit below. I should be ashamed. But, what can I say, I am not.

Whenever I was asked to rule on a point of law I was blessed with colleagues to whom I could send the questioner. Why offer second best when the best is close at hand? It is the heart not the *Halachah* (Jewish law) that interests me, and I confess that I am not really concerned with the details of tradition. Many would say I am not a good Jew, God forfend! But if a good Jew is one scrupulous with the law, then they are right.

Having said that, let me add this: It may just be that what you in America need is not a good Jew but a bad one like me. From what I hear about America, it is not so kosher a place that everyone is running to the rebbe to check a chicken's worthiness to be eaten. Me, I would rather you leave the bird alone. Perhaps we will talk about diet and *kashrut* (Jewish dietary laws) another time. All I mean to tell you is that my Judaism seeks only the heart of the teaching and the essence of the practice and leaves the details to others. I am not opposed to them. I am simply not drawn to them.

My Judaism is not of one camp or another. I am bored by labels. I owe allegiance only to God, Torah, and Israel. Let others debate and denounce. I haven't the mind for the first nor the stomach for the second. All I want is to be left alone to my study, my teaching, and my prayers. And my letters to you, my dear friend. I look forward to this exchange. The chance to continue our studies is a blessing to me. And I hope to you.

I will ask one thing further of you: do not destroy these letters. I head no *yeshivah* (school of Jewish learning), I have written no books, and I have chosen to work with so very few students that these letters may be my only legacy. I have never felt a need to have my thoughts outlive the mind that thinks them, and I still believe that the deepest teaching takes place in the face-to-face exchange of teacher and student. But you and I are not permitted this luxury, and something tells me that our situation will not be unique.

There will soon come a time when our people will be ignorant of our teachings, and confused about who they are. They will be troubled, and like the Simple Son of the *Haggadah* (the Passover prayer book) they will not even know what to ask. Perhaps you will be their voice, raising their questions that they may read my answers when the time arises. But that is out of our hands. All we can do is learn from each other. I eagerly await your next letter.

B'Shalom (in peace)

JUDAISM

My dearest Aaron Hershel,

You are quite right that we need to begin at the beginning. A new land, a new start. But as to your suggestion of "a new Judaism," who is to say? That is not my intent. My intent is just to answer your questions.

So, the question is "What is Judaism?" You know, of course, the Talmud's section on defining Judaism (*Makkot* 23b): Rabbi Simlai began by saying that the 613 *mitzvot* (commandments) were reduced to 11 by King David (Psalm 15), to six by Isaiah (Isaiah: 33:15), and then to three by Micah (Micah: 6:8). Isaiah further reduced them to two: "Keep judgment and righteousness." Amos came and reduced them to one: "Seek Me and live" (Amos: 5:4). Habbakuk proposed an alternative: "The Righteous live by faith" (Habbakuk: 2:4).

And I am certain you remember Hillel's famous reply to the Gentile who demanded he teach all of Torah while standing on one foot: "Do not do to others what you would not want done to yourself. That is the whole of Torah. The rest is commentary. Now go and study it" (*Shabbat* 31a).

I am partial to these one foot Judaisms. They are simple, direct, and profound. And they leave us free to shape a Jewish life around principle rather than tradition. I am not opposed to tradition, God forbid, but I do not think it superior to principle. On the contrary, tradition is our record of the way our ancestors lived these principles in the past. We should see them as catalysts to our own creativity and not as fixed forms to be imitated. This already is *treif* (not kosher, heretical) thinking on my part and I do not share this with my peers, but the teacher should not pretend before the student.

So here is my one foot Judaism: Judaism is the Jewish people's ancient and, God willing, ongoing effort to make *tikkun* and *teshuvah*. The rest is commentary. Now go and study it.

What do you think? On a par with Amos and Hillel? Probably not. Yerachmiel is no Habbakuk. But it is what I believe. Judaism is simply tikkun and teshuvah. Of course now I must be clear as to what I mean by tikkun and teshuvah.

Tikkun means "repair." The great saint and kabbalist Isaac Luria, peace be upon him (1534–1572), was the first to use this term in a spiritual way. He believed that when God set out to create the world, God, being infinite, had to contract in order to make room for what would become the finite world. God intended to pour the divine energy into specially constructed vessels that would form the foundation of creation. Yet God erred, so to speak, in the construction of these vessels and when the divine light entered them they shattered, spilling God, as it were, all over the cosmos.

These shattered fragments of God became trapped in *klippot* (shells) and these became embedded in the world you and I inhabit. Reb Luria taught that it was the task of the Jew to free these trapped sparks of God and return them to God by treating all things with utmost reverence and respect. Since the sparks were scattered across the world, the Jews would have to be scattered across the world. Our loss of Israel and our holy Temple in Jerusalem was not a punishment for our disobedience to God, but essential to God's plan. Who among us would have left the Holy Land of our own free will? No one! So God had the Romans push us out. What appeared to us as a loss of holiness, turns out in Luria's mind to be the way to holiness.

As you know, his understanding spoke to so many of our people. Luria's teaching replaced the horror of exile with the hope for redemption. And hope is the sap of life; without hope there is only lifeless form.

But, I will tell you, Aaron Hershel, that I do not believe Reb Luria meant us to take this teaching literally. Or, if he did, I for one cannot do so. What Luria saw as a process happening in God and the world, I see as a process happening only in our minds.

Did God really shrink to make room for creation? No! God is infinite. Can the infinite become finite? Of course not; the infinite includes the finite. What happens is not that God shrinks, but that the *Neshamah*, the ego, imagines a distant God to allow for the illusion of a separate self. And, once it has established itself as separate it goes about exploiting others in order to maintain its selfish delusion.

This, the Neshamah's rejection of the fundamental unity of all life in, with, and as God is to me the real understanding of the breaking of the vessels. The ego was meant to be a way of knowing God in the relative and finite world of seemingly separate things. But it came to identify so closely with this world that it could no longer place itself in the larger context of the unity of all things in God. Do not think I am saying ego is bad or that we should eliminate it. Ego is vital to our daily functioning in the world. We need a self to interact with the world. But we must not imagine that this self is anything more than a vessel of something far greater than it.

You and I and all living things are the vessels of God, the embodiment of *Elohut* (Godhead). In this we are one with God, yet we imagine ourselves to be separate from God and this creates in us the idea of brokenness. The brokenness of the world starts as a process in the mind, but it doesn't end there. We go about the world breaking it up into smaller and smaller segments, each often at war with the rest, without ever realizing we are warring with ourselves.

Tikkun is the process of putting things back together again.

There are two kinds of tikkun corresponding to the two kinds of brokenness we humans imagine. The first is called *tikkun hanefesh*, repairing the soul. The second is called *tikkun haolam*, repairing the world. Both must occur if we are to set things right, and neither takes precedence over the other. Indeed they are two ends of the same rope.

We make tikkun hanefesh when we end the delusion of separateness that keeps us feeling alienated from God and creation. The truth is that God is creation. There are not two realities, the divine and the natural. If this were so, God would not be infinite. God's infinity includes and transcends the finite world. There is only one reality that manifests in different ways. It is all God. Tikkun hanefesh is awakening to the fact that you and I and all things are one in, with, and as God.

We make tikkun haolam when we engage the world with justice and compassion, what I call godliness. Tikkun haolam is repairing the damage we do to life when we engage it unjustly and cruelly. Tikkun haolam is ending the violence that comes with seeking to control others, repairing the rifts between people, and between people and nature, and treating each other and all life with the utmost respect and care.

Tikkun hanefesh and tikkun haolam are two sides of the same coin. You cannot do one without doing the other: to end the divisions and violence around you, you must also end the divisions and violence within you. This is what Hillel meant when he said "If I am not for myself who will be for me?" This is tikkun hanefesh. "But if I am only for myself, what am I?" This is tikkun haolam. "And if not now, when?" (*Pirke Avot*) Tikkun of either type can be done only in the present. The past and future are beyond our reach. If you repair your world and your soul you must do so by entering fully into the present moment.

How do you do this? Through the practice of *teshuvah*. So many people now use the word to refer to a return to *Halachah* (Jewish law) and traditional ways of Jewish living but I use it differently.

Teshuvah means returning to God and godliness. When your mind is caught up in the delusion of separateness it is distracted from the present. The deluded mind dwells on the past or imagines the future, but is never at home in the present. Why? Because the delusion of separateness cannot be maintained in the present. Since separation is a delusion of the mind, it is imagined in the mind, and the mind cannot imagine in the present. Imagination is of the past or the future, never the present. We cannot imagine the here and now, we can only engage it. Teshuvah is returning the mind to the present, to God, for God is the eternal present; tikkun returns us to godliness, engaging each moment with the utmost respect and care. If you are interested we can discuss just how this is done, but in any case this is what I think Judaism is: tikkun and teshuvah.

I can almost hear your objections! What about God, What about Torah, What about Israel, What about *Shabbat* and *Yontif* (the Sabbath and Holy Days)? I am not ignoring these, and, if you ask, I will be happy to explore them with you. But we are talking about a one foot Judaism. Hillel, too, did not mention Shabbat. He said all the rest is commentary; now go and study it. I will say no less: Judaism is returning to God and godliness. All the rest is commentary. Come, let us study it.

B'Shalom

WHO IS A JEW?

My dearest Aaron Hershel,

Have I ever thought about sailing to Palestine? Yes, I have dreamed about living in the Holy Land. I would visit the burial places of our ancient mothers and fathers. I would pray at the graves of our teachers. I would let the past infuse me with its spirit. But my work is here with my students.

I share your letters with them and also my responses. They are more interested in your adventures than in my teaching. This we can get anytime, they tell me, but America is something else entirely. They imagine themselves selling horses as you now do. And they asked me to suggest to you that you pack books for sale on the backs of these horses so that you can sell wisdom along with the beasts. So, I pass it on.

I myself have never ridden a horse, though as a child I would imagine that I owned the horses of the Baal Shem Tov, those that could travel great distances in moments. Now that I am old I still believe in the horses of the *Besht* (an acronym for Baal Shem Tov), but I no longer desire to be anywhere but here.

Your last letter troubled me a little. It follows naturally from our discussion on what is Judaism, but you spoke of discord among Jews over, of all things, who is a Jew. What is the confusion? And what prompts the question? Are Gentiles sneaking into *tallitot* and *tefillin* (prayer shawls and phylacteries) and trying to pass themselves off as Jews?

I am sorry. I do not mean to make light of your question. Let me answer it honestly. To my mind a Jew is a person who identifies as a Jew, who makes Jewish culture his or her primary vehicle for celebration and meaning, who upholds the values of Torah, and who practices tikkun and teshuvah.

I will take up each of these in turn, but first let me reply to what you must be thinking as you read this paragraph: What about being born to a Jewish mother?

For centuries this has been the determining factor of who is a Jew. I do not mean to ignore it. I only question its value. Between you and me, and I think I will not share this with the others, what matters to me is not who your mother was, but what you yourself do. So what if your mother is a Jew? So what if your mother is a devout and pious Jew? If you yourself ignore the Sabbath and the Torah, if you deny God and make no effort to be godly, in what meaningful way are you a Jew?

It would be as if Fivel Lipshitz, the tailor's son who sells firewood from his wagon, were to suddenly call himself a tailor and start sewing suits. The boy cannot count to ten, let alone measure a caftan sleeve. I could imagine saying to him, "Fivel, can you cut cloth well?" No, he would tell me. "Well, can you sew a straight stitch?" No, again, he would say. "Tell me, can you hem a cuff or let out a pair of pants?" No, for a third time. "Then how is it you presume to call yourself a tailor?" My mother is a tailor so I am tailor. Can you imagine such nonsense? And yet that is exactly what we are saying about being Jewish!

Listen to me, Aaron Hershel. Bend near to this page as if I were about to whisper in your ear. It doesn't matter what your mother is or what your father is. It matters who you are. And just so we are clear, I would rather you marry a Gentile who would live as a Jew, than a Jew who lived as a Gentile.

There, I said it. So? Flog me. But what good is it if you marry a Jew and together you abandon Judaism? Will your children—they should be many, strong, healthy, and wise—will your children be good Jews if they are raised without Judaism? Yes, they will be Jews because their mother's blood is Jewish. But so what? They will be non-Jewish Jews, Gentiles who have Jewish ancestors.

But if you marry a good woman who admires our faith and our ways, and who is willing to learn and adapt, and who will help you raise children strong in Torah and their faith in God, then you have married well. And if she wished, I would swim to America and make her a Jew myself. And if she didn't wish? I would embrace your children as my own: Jews from a Jewish father, raised in a Jewish home with Jewish hearts and Jewish heads.

Yes, I think I will keep this just between the two of us. Too strong, maybe.

Back to my definition. A Jew is four things.

First, a Jew is a person who willingly identifies as a Jew. What kind of Jew is a person who says he is a Catholic? Should I count him in a *minyan* (prayer quorum)? No. If you don't want to be known as a Jew, fine. (I am speaking in general and not, of course, to you personally, my dear Hershele) Then, to my mind, you are not a Jew. Will the Cossacks care one whit about what you call yourself when they come charging in thirsty for Jewish blood? No. But I am not a Cossack and I will not let them define for me who is a Jew. So they will kill a few Christians along with the Jews. I assure you, they won't mind.

Second, a Jew is a person who honors the joys and sorrows of life with the traditions of Judaism. When a boy is born there should be a *bris* (circumcision). When a daughter marries there should be a *chuppah* (wedding canopy) and a *ketubah* (wedding contract). When there is a death there should be a *shivah* (mourning period). These are examples, you understand. There is so much more to Judaism than these. But my point is that being a Jew means rooting your life in, though not necessarily regulating your life by, Jewish tradition.

Third, a Jew is a person who upholds the values of Torah. What values? One God who created one world and one humanity, and who demands that we treat each other, Jew and Gentile, with the utmost respect as beings created in the image and likeness of God, and who placed us in a garden which we were to maintain.

Fourth, a Jew is a person who practices tikkun and teshuvah. A Jew who does not work to repair the rifts in the world, both inner and outer, this person is a poor Jew. A Jew who does not do teshuvah, who does not attend to the present moment and engage it with godliness, this person, too, is a poor Jew.

I will not set forth the details here of how to be a Jew. Indeed, I am inclined to let people find their own way through mitzvot and halachah. But suffice it to say that as much as we call ourselves the Chosen People, it is becoming more and more clear to me that if we are to mean anything at all in this world we must become the Choosing People—people who choose to live by the principles and practices of tikkun and teshuvah: acting justly and compassionately toward all creatures, and cultivating the awareness of all selves as a manifestation of God.

My best to you and your horses.

B'Shalom

GOD

My dearest Aaron Hershel,

You ask me of God, to define the Nameless, to place in your palm the secret of the One who spoke and the world came to be. And here it is: God is All.

I am tempted to stop with this, to close this letter, sign my name, and leave you with this simple truth. Yet I fear you will not understand. Know from the first that all that follows is but an elaboration of the simple fact that God is All.

What does it mean to be All? God is the sole Reality. God is the Source of all things and their Substance. There is no thing or feeling or thought that is not from God, even the idea that there is no God! For this is what it is to be All: God must embrace even God's own negation.

Listen again: God is the Source and Substance of everything and its opposite. There is nothing outside of God. Thus we read: "I am God and there is none else" (Isaiah 45:5). Not simply that there is no other god but God, as our Moslem cousins say, but that there is nothing else but God, which is what their Sufi masters whisper to the initiated.

It rained heavily during the night, and our village is thick with mud. I walked to the *Beit Midrash* (House of Learning) this morning and stopped to watch a group of little children playing in a puddle of mud.

They sat in the puddle, oblivious to the damp, and made dozens of mud figures: houses, animals, and towers. From their talk it was clear that they imagined an identity for each: a story that told the figure's past and foretold its future. For a while the mud figures took on independence, a life separate and unique. But they are still just mud. Mud is their source, and mud is their substance. From the perspective of the children wrapped up in the play of separate figures their mud creations had separate selves. From the point of view of a casual observer it is clear that the separate self is an illusion, that in fact they are all just mud.

It is the same with us and God: "*Adonai* (the Lord) alone is God in heaven above and on earth below, there is none else" (Deuteronomy 4:39). *Ayn od*—there is none else—meaning that there is nothing else in heaven or on earth but God.

Can this be? When I look at the world I do not see God. I see trees of varying kinds, people of all types, houses, fields, lakes, cows, horses, chickens, and on and on. In this I am like the children at play seeing real figures and not simply mud.

Where in all this is God?

Some would argue that God is a divine spark inside each being, some would say only within human beings. Others would argue that God is above and outside creation. But I teach neither position. God is not inside or outside, God is the very thing itself! And when there is no thing, but only empty space? God is that as well.

I want you to remember two important words: *Yesh* and *Ayn,* form and emptiness. Yesh refers to the seeming separateness of things, each thing having its own form, its own boundary, its own separate existence. Ayn refers to the emptiness of things, to the fact that forms and boundaries are not real in and of themselves, but rather useful constructions of the mind. To feed myself I must be able to separate my mouth from your mouth. This ability creates the world of Yesh. But to love my neighbor as my self (Leviticus 19:18) I must be able to transcend that distinction and recognize a greater unity without form. This is Ayn.

And which is God, Yesh or Ayn? Both and neither!

Picture a bowl in your mind. Define the bowl. Is it just the clay that forms its walls? Or is it the empty space that fills with borscht? Without the space the bowl is useless. Without the walls the bowl is useless. So which is the bowl? The answer is both. To be a bowl it must have form and emptiness.

It is the same with God. For God to be God, for God to be All, God must manifest both as both form and emptiness. This teaching is called *shlemut*, the completeness of God. To be shlemut God must contain all opposites. God must be both Yesh and Ayn simultaneously.

I have recently found a wonderful analogy to explain this teaching of shlemut, God's completeness. It has to do with magnets. I know little about them but this: A magnet has two poles, one positive and one negative. A magnet cannot be otherwise and still be a magnet. The two poles go together and only when they are together can there be a magnet. Even if you cut the magnet in half and in half again, it will always manifest these two poles. No matter how small you slice the magnet, its very nature necessitates the duality of positive and negative poles.

Now think of God. Yesh and Ayn are the poles of God. God cannot be God without them, and they cannot be themselves without each other and God. This is what is meant by God's shlemut, God's wholeness. All opposites are contained in and necessitated by God. We will return to this truth over and over again for it explains the deepest mysteries.

But enough for now. I have sought to clarify and may have only confused. You asked a difficult question, made all the more difficult because the answer is so simple: God is All.

B'Shalom

CREATION

My dearest Aaron Hershel,

How wonderful to find your letter waiting for me this morning. I had not expected to hear from you so soon. It is always a delight. And your question! Why did God create the world? What is the purpose of creation?

Could you have started with anything smaller? Definitions we have, reasons why—that is another matter altogether. But you ask and I answer. That is how it is with us, and I am blessed to have you as my student.

Why did God create the world?

Because it is God's nature to manifest shlemut, divine wholeness and infinite possibility. Infinite possibility must include Yesh and Ayn, form and emptiness. You see, I told you that these words would return again and again. Everything can be understood through them.

Do not imagine God as a separate being apart from Creation who decides to create. God does not decide as we decide. God's will is only to fulfill God's nature. And God's nature is to manifest Yesh and Ayn. This is God's nature, this is what God is: The source and substance of all and nothing.

Recall my analogy of the magnets. Remember how the two poles, positive and negative, go together and only when they are together can there be a magnet? Can we say that the one pole precedes the other? Can we say that the one pole creates the other?

No. Each pole arises with the other. Its being depends upon the other. And vice versa. There is no first and second, there is no primacy of one over the other. There is only the two forever together. The magnet does not decide to make this happen; this is simply what the magnet is: two poles held in a greater unity. It is the nature of the magnet to hold these opposite poles in its greater unity; the magnet cannot be otherwise.

So, too, with God. Yesh and Ayn are the poles of God. God cannot be God without them, they cannot be themselves without each other and God. Thus all arise together. This is what is meant by God's shlemut, God's wholeness and completeness. The shlemut of God necessitates both Yesh and Ayn. The manifestation of Yesh and Ayn is what it means to be God.

Thus, those who tell you that our everyday world, the world we see from the perspective of Yesh, is illusory and without consequence are wrong. This world is of supreme value for it, no less than Ayn, is of God. Our world is fragile and impermanent, but it is the temporal and fleeting world of Yesh that is needed to reveal the timelessness of Ayn. And both are needed to express the completeness of God.

The sainted Aaron HaLevi Horowitz of Straosselje, (1776-1829) one of the early students of Hasidism and my teacher's teacher, taught: "The main point of creation is to reveal God's completeness from the opposite perspective." Unity in the midst of diversity. Creation happens because God cannot but be God. And to be God, God must manifest that which appears to be separate from God, the temporal world we call Yesh.

The unawakened human mind recognizes things only in contrast to other things. We know *I* only in relation to *Thou*, *good* only in relation to *evil*, *right* only in relation to *left*, *up* only in relation to *down*. The human mind rarely sees beyond these opposites to the greater unity that necessitates them. But the mind can awaken to greater unity, and in this lies the purpose of creation and humankind. The purpose of creation is to manifest the infinite God in the finite world. The purpose of humanity is to know that creation is a manifestation of God.

Why, then, did God create the heavens and the earth? There is no *why* to creation. Creation is because God is. Is there value in creation? Of course. For creation is the way God is God in time and space. Creation is holy in and of itself for in and of itself it is God. This is what God means when Torah says: "Be holy for I, the Source and Substance of All Form and Emptiness, am Holy" (Leviticus 19:2). Holiness is the natural state of reality. We are holy because God is holy, and we are God manifest in time and place. The Torah's command is to be true to our divine nature and to honor the divine nature of all things.

When God created humankind what did God say? "Let us create adam (earthling, *adam* from *adamah*, earth) in our image" (Genesis 1:26). Who is this *us*? Some say God was speaking as a king who refers to himself in the third person plural: We decree this and we decree that. Others say God was conversing with the angels. In the book of Proverbs we read that Wisdom was with God at creation so maybe God was consulting her. I have a problem with all of these.

First, God does not speak in the kingly manner elsewhere in Torah, so why here? Second, there is no mention of the creation of angels in Genesis, so why assume them? Third, there is no mention of Wisdom in Genesis either, so why assume she was there?

We don't have to *imagine* who God was speaking to. It is clear from the Torah that God was talking with the other beings that had just been created. God says let us make a being in our image after our likeness. And then God fashions adam from adamah, the earthen one from the earth. No other being was so fashioned. Only people. Why? To tell us that we are not alien to this world. To remind us that we come out of the earth and were not placed upon her.

What is the difference? When we imagine we are other than the mud and soil and plants and animals with whom we share this world we can imagine that we are superior. And if we are superior we can do with them whatever we choose. But if we know that we too are from the earth, then we will not feel superior. We will not walk upon the fields as victors seeking to impose our reign, but as children playing at the hem of their mother's skirt or sucking on her milk-filled breast.

I know you will counter by saying God gave us the whole of creation to subdue and use. But I would argue that this is an example of Torah failing to speak divine wisdom. It happens at times and we can speak at length about this if you wish. My point is that Torah speaks the word of God when that word unites rather than divides.

We find two opinions in Torah. One says that we are to subdue nature and rule over her. The other says that we are to honor her as our self, that we are to realize that "The earth is God's and the fullness thereof" (Exodus 30:20). Can there be even a doubt in your mind as to which is the true teaching? There is none in mine.

God speaks through Torah when Torah teaches us of our fundamental connection with the earth and all she bears. The trees and grasses, the wolves and bears, the oceans and seas— these are our brothers, our sisters, our cousins.

I am tempted to go more deeply into this. For the question of the purpose of creation leads, as it has already, directly into the purpose of humanity. I will resist the impulse to proceed, however, suspecting that I have caused enough confusion for one letter.

All I ask of you, my dear friend, is that you look to see if my words are not so. Look carefully about you and ponder: If creation is God manifest in time and place, what is the purpose of humanity? I look forward to your insights.

B'Shalom

HUMANITY

My dearest Aaron Hershel,

When we began our correspondence I did not know what to expect either from you or from myself. Would I be able to answer your questions in a manner that furthered your knowledge and deepened your ability to question? Or would I simply overwhelm you with information and drown out your ability to see for yourself? Your recent letter suggests you can learn and think. I had asked you the question: What is the purpose of humanity? You answered well. Let me add some thoughts of my own.

Following the twofold nature of God as both Yesh and Ayn there are two ways of knowing the world. From the perspective of Yesh, the world is a collection of diverse, separate and transient beings competing with one another for survival. From the perspective of Ayn, the world is a homogeneous oneness without time, space, and separate beings. To become overly attached to either perspective is to miss God's shlemut.

God as God, however, cannot "know" this wholeness for "knowing" requires that one is separate from that which is known, and nothing is separate from God. Yet the shlemut of God requires that knowing. Thus it is God's nature to manifest beings capable of perceiving both form and emptiness, and that which includes both, God. The human being is among those beings.

We have been created to know the greater unity of God. We are not here to amass fortunes. We are not here to win wars or competitions. We are not here to earn rewards or make for ourselves a great name. We are here to know God, and through our knowing to effect God's self-realization and self-knowing. We are not an accident. We are a necessary extension of God's greater wholeness.

How do I know this? Torah reveals it to me. Look at the creation of humankind in Genesis. In chapter one we learn that men and women are created in the image and likeness of God (Genesis 1:27), but it doesn't tell us how or why. We learn both in chapter two. Yes, I know that the two stories are not the same, and we can argue forever in hopes of reconciling them, but this is an argument from which I will refrain. I am interested in the accuracy of the message not the *meshugas* (craziness) of the medium.

So what do we learn in chapter two? "Neither trees nor herbs were on the earth for God had not sent rain upon the earth and there was no human to work the soil," (Genesis 2:5). Here we learn the why of humanity: our job is to till the soil.

What? Are we all to be farmers? You see, I can read your mind. This is what you are thinking, is it not? And, no, we are not all to be farmers. Torah is telling us something far more profound.

To understand what Torah is teaching we must ask two questions: What does it mean to till the soil? and What is the soil we humans are to till?

Tilling the soil means breaking up the hard-packed earth and allowing it to breathe. What soil are we talking about? The soil that is humanity: "God formed the human from the dust of the earth, and He blew into its nostrils the breath of life; and the human became conscious and alive" (Genesis 2:7).

Can you see the teaching here? We are the soil that needs tilling. We become hard, dry, airless, and lifeless. Our task is to bring breath back into the soil just as God breathed breath into the soul. Bringing breath back to the soil of humanity means to open ourselves up to the world, engage life in a manner that promotes life.

Compare two other biblical teachings: The tower of Babel and the heavenly ladder of Jacob. In the case of the tower, the people of earth unite to build "a tower with its top in the sky in order to make a name for ourselves" (Genesis 11:4). God rejects their efforts. In the case of the ladder, Torah tells us Jacob "had a dream; a ladder was set on the ground and its top reached to the sky, and angels of God were going up and down on it," (Genesis 28:12). God blesses Jacob.

Now note: both the tower of Babel and the ladder of Jacob reached up from the earth "with its top in the sky." The wording is identical! So why the different reactions from God?

While both the tower and the ladder link earth and heaven, in Babel the people sought to escape the one and rise to the other. In Jacob's dream the two are unified through the two-way flow of divine energy, the angels. God rejects anything short of completeness.

So now you must ask yourself this: If the purpose of humanity is to realize both Yesh and Ayn and thereby reveal the shlemut of God, what does that mean to me as an individual? How can I fulfill my destiny as a human being and realize God in my own life?

That is the work of tikkun and teshuvah. Tikkun haolam honors the shlemut of God in the outer world, making for harmony among different peoples, nations, even species. Tikkun hanefesh honors the shlemut of God in the inner world, bringing harmony to the conflicting urges of body and mind. Teshuvah is returning the mind to God. When your awareness is on the present rather than the past or the future you are open to what is. And what is is God.

We must talk at some point about how to practice teshuvah in your daily life, and we will. But not just yet.

B'Shalom

EVIL

My dearest Aaron Hershel,

I am pleased you have such a deep mind and are willing to wrestle with my often jumbled thoughts. These letters have given me a chance to sort out my thinking somewhat, but I still have a long way to go. But of course the real joy of your last letter was the word about the impending marriage between you and Sarah Leah!

You had not mentioned that there was a woman in your life, and so to read of your engagement was such a surprise. There is no need to explain why you kept her a secret. I was in love once, and preferred to keep my feelings quiet until I was certain of them. I did not wish to become burdened with feelings I did not feel simply because I once loudly announced that I felt them.

When I was ready I spoke to Faige's father, may they both rest in peace. It was not a pretty sight. I hope your experience was better than mine. I had so little to offer. I wanted to be a scholar, he wanted someone to go into business. I wanted to teach, he wanted someone who could sell. I could never have convinced him. I think it was his daughter that turned him in my favor. She had that power over him. Over me as well. We should talk about death and grief some time.

But not now. Now you want to talk about evil. If the task of humanity is to know God, how is it that we experience such evil? Could there be a more difficult query? And yet I can tell by the way you write of evil that you grasp much.

You are right to go back to first principles, to the dual nature of God as Yesh and Ayn. Good and evil are twins birthed by the singular source and substance of all reality. Thus we read: "I am the Source and Substance of Reality, there is nothing else. I form light and create darkness, I make peace and create evil. I, the Source and Substance of All, do all this," (Isaiah 45:6–7).

Evil is not the opposite of God, evil is a manifestation of God. What then is the purpose of evil? Why does God allow evil to exist? You answer wisely: It is not a matter of purpose and allowing, it is a matter of the unconditional nature of God's shlemut. If God is God, God must contain all possibility, everything and its opposite. Good and evil are but two of the infinite possibilities of God.

All this you understood on your own. Excellent. I cannot tell you the joy I feel at the mind you have. So now let us go a bit deeper, for while the possibility of evil is of God and therefore necessary to the divine shlemut, the various manifestations of evil are not always necessary.

I shall speak of two types of evil: necessary evil and unnecessary evil. The first refers to the simple sorrows of everyday life: accident, sickness, old age, death. The second refers to the wickedness we humans inflict upon each other and the world around us.

The first is necessary or natural because it arises from the fleeting and transient nature of the world of Yesh, our everyday world of seemingly separate selves. Suffering, old age, death, accident, natural disaster, all the pain that arises from the passing of time and circumstance—these are called evil by those of us who imagine ourselves to be separate and permanent beings. They are called evil because they thwart our desires and, in the case of death, shatter the façade of our own permanence. In fact, most of what we call evil is simply the order of things in time and space. For all the pain this causes, there is no real evil here.

The proper response to the natural suffering caused by necessary evil is to grieve and accept. Free from the illusion of separation and permanence we are able to embrace the natural suffering of impermanent reality with a deep sense of grace and perhaps even humor. We understand that sickness, accidents, the ending of relations both business and personal, old age, and death are all part of the nature of Yesh, and while we do what we can to minimize these we do not pretend that we can eliminate them.

One who understands the nature of Yesh opens to a deep calm that allows one to feel fully and respond constructively to whatever life brings.

There is a story about Rabbi Akiva who was once lost in a shipwreck at sea. He alone survived, and when asked how he did so he said, "Whenever a wave arouse I bent into it." He bent to the wave and it washed over him. This is how we are to live in the world: bending into what happens and allowing it to wash over us rather than to sweep us away.

So much for dealing with the natural or necessary evil of the world. Let us turn to what I call real or unnecessary evil. Unnecessary evil is the evil we humans do when we refuse to fulfill the dual human obligation of teshuvah and tikkun, returning to God and repairing the world with godliness. Real evil happens when we act in ways that disrupt unity, that foster discord, that promote division, hatred, and fear.

How does this evil arise? Real evil arises from an inability to get beyond Neshamah, the hard-packed ego we are supposed to till, and to love another as oneself.

Last year the winter was harsher than most. The cold was unbearable, especially for the aged and very young. There were some in our village who called the cold evil, but this is foolish. It was winter and it was cold. Nothing more. But there was evil that winter. The evil came in the decision to raise the price of firewood so high that many of us could not afford to purchase enough to warm our homes.

My point is this: Real evil is an act of self-gratification that disregards the worth and holiness of other beings. Real evil is generated by a self out of touch with life, a self cut off from the oneness of God and the compassion, love, and justice that oneness commands.

What is the antidote to such evil? Tilling the soil of self and selfishness; letting in the breath of life that awakens the self to its true nature as a being created in the image and likeness of God whose purpose is to serve life through love. Unless and until the self is broken open before the Greater Unity of God there is no hope for real compassion, justice, or love. And how do we make for self-opening? Through the practice of teshuvah and tikkun, continually returning our attention to God and our behavior to godliness.

Look for yourself and see.

B'Shalom

HUMAN NATURE

My dearest Aaron Hershel,

It is good that you are aware of your own personal capacity for evil, your own ability to rationalize selfishness and excuse wickedness. Admitting this is the first step to controlling it. Now you are concerned that we humans are innately evil, something you heard from a Christian neighbor.

You are right to be concerned. But you are wrong to equate what I said with what you have heard. Talk of original sin is totally alien to Judaism, though it is a good way for me to introduce the Jewish view of human nature.

As I understand it, and I admit to having but a surface knowledge of this teaching, it is the position of the Church, both Catholic and Protestant, that the sin of Adam and Eve is carried by all humanity. Each of us is born bearing that original sin of the original human couple. And the only way to free ourselves from this sin is to believe in Jesus of Nazareth as the only begotten son of God, for in exchange for our belief he will cleanse us of our sin.

While I am in no position to claim the Church is wrong, I can say quite simply that nowhere in the story of Adam and Eve does Torah speak of sin. True, the first couple disobeyed the command of God, but this is not called a sin in Torah.

Read your Torah carefully and tell me why Eve violated the only commandment God had laid upon her. "And the woman perceived that the tree was good for eating, and that it was a delight to the eyes, and that the tree was desirable as a means to wisdom, and she took of its fruit and ate...." (Genesis 3:6).

Torah does not waste words. Why not simply say: the woman ate? That would have made the point if the point was eating. But the point is not eating. The point is why she ate.

First she sees that the tree is good for eating, but she does not eat. Then she sees that it is beautiful to look upon, but she does not eat. Only when she realizes that it is the source of wisdom does she eat.

Meaning? It is not desire or beauty that compels the human being, but wisdom, and in quest of wisdom we are willing to sacrifice everything. We are not driven by sin, but by the quest to know. A wonderful myth! A timeless message! So where is the original sin in this?

Jews do not see the eating of the fruit of knowledge of good and evil as the fall of humankind, but as its first step toward fulfilling its destiny. Life in Eden would never have resulted in the awakening of a mind capable of realizing Yesh and Ayn as the two poles of God. Eve and Adam had to leave paradise if they were to grow.

A second difference between Judaism and Christianity: We do not believe that we need the intervention of another to effect our getting right with God. We do not need faith in a messiah to mend our relationship with God. God is always waiting for us. All we need do is return, make teshuvah, pay attention to the present, and discover the Presence. Teshuvah and tikkun, returning to God and godliness, are totally up to us. It is a matter of will not faith.

Of all the differences between these two faiths, it is the matter of teshuvah that is the greatest. Christians do not believe in teshuvah. Ultimately only the Son of God can bring you back to God. There is nothing so un-Jewish as this. Our messiah returns us to Israel, our decision to make teshuvah returns us to God.

So when I say that human beings have the capacity for evil, I in no way mean to imply that we are born with some original sin that only a messiah can forgive.

Torah tells us clearly that we are created in the image of God, the One who is both Yesh and Ayn. As beings created in God's image, we too must contain both Yesh and Ayn. And so we do. In human beings Yesh and Ayn appear as *Yetzer haRah*, our capacity for evil, and *Yetzer haTov,* our capacity for good.

The human equivalent of the divine Ayn, the Yetzer haTov is that innate human capacity for unity. Yetzer haTov is our ability to bridge differences, to build community, to effect harmony. Without the balancing vision of Yetzer haRah, however, it is also the tendency to erase diversity, to ignore uniqueness, to work toward a homogeneity that can be quite dull and even lifeless. Thus our sages taught that without the Yetzer haRah a person would not marry, or build a home, or raise a family, for these rely on our ability to differentiate and celebrate diversity (*Genesis Rabbah* 9:7).

Yetzer haRah, despite its unfortunate label, is the human capacity to honor differences, the human equivalent to the divine Yesh. Yetzer haRah sees differences where the Yetzer haTov sees sameness. Yetzer haRah sees every living thing as an entity unto itself, as unique and apart from the whole. Yetzer haTov sees no separate forms or beings, but the formless unity of God.

Why call Yetzer haRah *rah,* evil? Because without the balancing insight of the Yetzer haTov, the Yetzer haRah's insistence on separate self and independence pits one life against another, destroying any hope for community, justice and compassion, all of which rely on the notion that we are at root one.

Yet a world without Yetzer haRah, a world run solely by Yetzer haTov is no less evil. For without the ability to recognize and respect individual differences, justice is reduced to conformity, compassion to pity and community to uniformity. A healthy world needs both Yetzer haRah and its welcoming of and respect for individuality, and Yetzer haTov with its insight into interdependence and harmony.

Let me try to set this in a more practical context.

When you walk in the forest and come upon an especially beautiful flower there is an immediate perception of beauty with no sense of *I* and *Thou,* self or flower. The selfless meeting with the flower arises from Yetzer haTov. No sense of separation exists. No "I" that sees or flower that is seen. There is only a sense of wonder and beauty. The self and the flower are one in Ayn, divine emptiness. Our initial encounter with the world of Yesh involves no sense of separate self, no "I." There is only experience, awareness, knowing, but no self who experiences or is aware or knows. In a sense one can say that our initial encounter with Yesh is from the perspective of Ayn.

Almost immediately, however, the Yetzer haRah, the inclination for separation, is activated and we say to ourselves: "Ah, what a beautiful flower!" At that moment self is born. As soon as the flower's beauty is known there must be a self that knows it. It is the Yetzer haRah, the inclination to discriminate between self and other, that interprets the experience and posits a self. We go from simple wonder and beauty to "I see the beautiful flower."

Please do not imagine that one way of meeting is good and the other bad. Seeing the flower through the eyes of Yetzer haTov is no more a choice we make then is seeing the flower through the eyes of Yetzer haRah. Both are completely natural and necessary. This is simply the way we encounter the world. To encounter the world fully means to allow for and to understand both ways of seeing.

If you look closely at your meeting with the flower, you will also see that the initial selfless encounter is timeless. There is only the immediacy of beauty. As soon as the Yetzer haRah intervenes with a sense of self and other—I see a beautiful flower—time enters the equation.

Time and self are intimately connected. Indeed, the one cannot be without the other. That is why the experience of Ayn appears timeless. Self, time, form, and being are all of the same aspect of reality.

End one and you end them all. The human cry for eternal life is but a misguided glimpse into the timeless nature of self-emptying into Ayn.

If the experience associated with the "I" is a pleasant one, the self seeks to hold on to it. If it is a negative one, the self seeks to avoid it. Both holding and avoiding lead to unnecessary suffering, because both fly in the face of the transitory nature of reality as experienced by self in time.

The world of Yesh is fleeting. It is the world of time, change, impermanence, and death. To seek to control your experiences in this world, either by clinging or avoiding, is to set yourself up for needless disappointment. And yet this is precisely what the Yetzer haRah tends to do.

As long as you live under the dictates of the Yetzer haRah, the illusion of separateness and independence, you will forever seek to control what happens to you. You will strive to hold on to pleasantness and avoid pain. You will go to great lengths to fulfill your desires, and when you are frustrated in your efforts, which must happen since you are not in control of what life brings, you become angry or despairing or both. As long as you identify solely with the Yetzer haRah you will be unbalanced, selfish, isolated, anxious, and prone to all sorts of physical and mental diseases.

When you understand the nature of God and yourself as a manifestation of God, you will allow form to be form and emptiness to be emptiness and each to embrace the other without rancor or upset.

Think on this and write me when you can.

B'Shalom

TORAH

My dearest Aaron Hershel,

You are right to say there is much to digest in my last letter, and I will honor your request to move on to something a bit less abstract. Indeed, I am happy to discuss your next question and investigate with you the nature of Torah.

As you know, we Jews use Torah, which means Teaching, in many ways. It refers to the Five Books of Moses, what we call the *Chumash*, from *chamesh*, the Hebrew word for "five." We say Torah when we mean the complete Bible. We even speak of a given rabbi's teaching as rabbi so-and-so's Torah. I will restrict my thoughts to the Torah as Chumash.

Of course, you know very well that I have a different understanding of Torah than most. But I would caution you against calling my teachings a philosophy. I cannot pretend to have worked out the details of my ideas sufficiently to call them that. They are just the musings of an old man with too much time on his hands, and too much pride in his heart.

So what is Torah? Torah is the Jewish people's diary of its early encounters with God. It is a blend of myth, legend, history, ethics, and timeless revelation. It tells us where we came from, and where perhaps we ought to be going, and offers guidance from those who have taken up the journey before us. It is a book whose meanings are as numerous as the people who dare to uncover them. It is my constant companion. Where my colleagues turn to Jewish law for guidance in God's ways, I turn to Torah for insight and meaning into life and how to live it.

I know I need to explain all of this, but I want to make something very clear before I do. I want you to know what Torah is not. Torah is not a science book, nor is it a blueprint for social mores. I say this because so many mistake it for just these things. When Torah speaks to us of the six days of creation, are we to imagine six sunsets? The sun itself wasn't even created until the third day! When Torah says we are to murder a rebellious child, are we to take that as the highest expression of human values? Of course not. We have to read Torah in the context of its time and its culture, so that we can free the timeless message that is meant for all times and all peoples.

Thank God we Jews have never restricted ourselves to a literal interpretation of Torah. We have taught for centuries that each word, each letter, has multiple meanings and at least four levels of interpretation. There is *pshat*, the surface reading of the text. There is *remez*, the allegorical reading. There is *drash* the metaphorical reading. And there is *sod*, the mystical reading. While no reading can violate the plain sense of the text, that is to say we cannot argue that God planted a rose bush rather than a tree at the center of *Gan Eden* (Garden of Eden), we are free to explore the many dimensions of just what Eden and the tree might mean for us in our time and circumstance. It is this freedom to interpret that keeps the Torah alive. And it is the Torah's capacity to speak to us in our time and circumstance that keeps us in dialogue with it.

While Torah may reflect the science and morals of its time, it is not meant to be a book of timeless scientific truths nor moral values. What it is is a blending of myth, legend, history, law, poetry, and timeless wisdom.

What are the myths of Torah? The stories of *Bereshit* (Genesis) from creation to the call of *Avraham Aveinu* (Abraham our Father). These are wonder tales of the earliest humans. Are they true? Yes. Are they factual? No.

Myth is often the poetic expression of deep truth. Myth is meant to be read over and again, knowing that each time you read it you will find something new in it. A myth is a kind of mirror, reflecting the unconscious truths of your own life back to your conscious mind. Myths should be read and honored as great tools for self-knowing. But to insist that they are historical fact is to twist the mirror and distort the message.

Legend refers to the stories of our ancestors from the call of Avraham Aveinu to the birth of *Moshe Rabbeinu* (Moses, our rabbi). These too are true even if they are not historical fact. The message of these legends has to do with the way we are to conduct ourselves in the world. Does it matter if Avraham really argued with God over the fate of Sodom? Not at all! What matters is that Avraham dared to hold even God accountable to the principle of justice. "Should not the Judge of all the world do justly?" (Genesis 30:20) Do you know what a revolution that was in human thought?

Before Avraham gods were all powerful. People quaked in fear of their power. With Avraham we are given a new way to approach God: as friend and as partner. And as friends we are obligated to warn each other when we think the other is about to do something wrong. So Avraham argues with God. To save Sodom? Maybe. But to save God, absolutely!

These legends may reflect history. It is fine by me if they do and fine by me if they do not. Their message transcends the facts of history.

Of course there is real history in Torah. The settling of Israel, the warring of nations, and the reign of kings. This is the history of our people, and we should know it. Without memory a nation cannot stand. And there is law, which tells us the values and virtues our ancient ancestors upheld. And there is wondrous poetry in Torah: the Psalms, the Song of Songs, but none of these touches the power of the divine revelations Torah contains.

What do I mean by revelation? Revelation is the teachings that reflect the foundation principle of all Judaism: *l'chayyim*, for life. Let me explain.

Our sages taught that Avraham our Father kept all the laws of the Torah. How is this possible since he lived centuries before the giving of the Torah at Mount Sinai? One sage taught that Avraham lived by a single principle that underlies all of Torah. Avraham performed acts that would deepen our love of God and creation, and refrained from acts that would lessen our love of God and creation. In this he lived the foundational principle of Judaism. The acts that deepened our love of God and creation are acts in touch with l'chayyim.

So how can we apply this to our search for revelation in Torah itself? Any teaching found in Torah that lifts you out of your self–centeredness, brings you closer to God, and places you in a godly relationship with the world—that is revelation based in l'chayyim. Any teaching found in Torah that focuses on selfishness, distances you from God, or lifts you above the world and places you in conflict with it, that is not l'chayyim, but the workings of ego.

If you are paying attention, my dear Hershele, you will realize that what I am saying is not for the timid. Torah is not from God, but from human beings. It contains divine wisdom, but also human folly. The wisdom is the voice of God's love, and speaks for the principle of l'chayyim. The folly is the voice of human fear, and speaks for the principle of death, violence, division, exploitation, and the rest of the madness that we humans can inflict upon one another.

So, for example, when Torah says we are not to take advantage of the powerless—the widow, the orphan, the stranger, the blind—it is speaking from love of life; this is divine revelation. But when it commands us to murder the Amalekites, then it speaks from fear and is no longer a revelation.

So when it comes to God's commands in Torah you must be very careful to discern which are l'chayyim and which are not; which speak from love and which speak from fear. Only the words of l'chayyim and love can be counted as timeless revelations of God. The rest are the madness of ego masquerading as God.

Please do not imagine that I am suggesting you ignore the ego's Torah, the Torah that speaks from fear. This would be a terrible error. All of Torah is to be studied, but for different reasons. Study the Torah of Love to learn how to act. Study the Torah of Fear to learn how not to act. Both Torahs speak to you because both love and fear are a part of you. Honor the first by imitating it. Honor the second by recognizing it in yourself and then controlling it.

I wonder if I am making matters clearer or more confusing for you? You will tell me, I am sure. But before I close this letter, let me answer two other questions that may be on your mind: Why and how are we to study Torah?

Why study Torah? Study Torah because it mirrors the whole spectrum of human truth and behavior from the most sacred to the most sinister. Study Torah because you can see in the violence of our ancestors the evil of which you yourself are capable. Study Torah because you can see in the saintliness of our ancestors the spiritual heights to which you can aspire. Study Torah because you can see in the sorrow and repentance of our ancestors the way to correct error by living justly and with compassion.

How to study Torah?

Read the myths for the grand themes they convey. Read them as if they were dreams you dreamed the night before. See yourself in the myth, and the myth as a map of your life. Ask yourself how the myth sets a course for godliness and see if you can align yourself with its compass.

Read the legends for the personal virtues they embody. While not every hero and heroine in the Torah is a saint, each speaks in his or her way to the struggles of living a life devoted to godliness. See in their lives hints as to how to live your life. Their deeds instruct us, even when they do so by making plain the evil we need to avoid.

Read the history for the civic values upon which our ancestors' society was based. Here, too, there is good and evil. Here, too, we find great leaps forward to godliness and equally great falls into wickedness. Be clear as to which is which, and honor them both by embodying the first and working to control the second.

Read the law for the principles it sought to embody. Do not accept the law as binding simply because it was once so. Ask yourself if it furthers the principle of l'chayyim or not. If it does, find a way to adhere to it, in spirit if not in letter. If not, note it for what it is, and do not become entangled in it.

Read the poetry for its sheer beauty and depth of passion. Rabbi Akiva taught that all Torah is holy, and that the Song of Songs is the holy of holies. The Song of Songs is the ultimate poetic expression in Torah. It, along with Psalms articulates the full range of human feelings and striving. Poetry can say things prose cannot. Indulge yourself in the power of our people's poems as you would indulge yourself in a fine meal.

Read the teachings for those timeless truths that speak to all humankind. Again, not everything in Torah is true or holy, loving or kind. Much is false, fearful, violent, and even cruel. Do not flee from the negative or seek to hide in the positive. Listen to the wisdom Torah contains, just be careful to follow the path of love even as you work to curtail the dictates of fear.

B'Shalom

MITZVOT

My dearest Aaron Hershel,

I am not surprised that your last letter asked about my opinion of *mitzvot* (Jewish practices). My comments on Torah made it clear that I do not hold every word or law sacred, and therefore you are right to question me regarding the laws that are derived from Torah. But do not think I am about to dismiss mitzvot out of hand. After all, we both grew up with *tallit* and *tefillin* (prayer shawl and phylacteries). Am I now suggesting we abandon them? God forbid! I could no more start a day without *tefillah* (prayer) and tefillin, than I could start a day without breathing. And yet I am not pleased with the way mitzvot are taught or even how they are understood.

We are taught that mitzvah, religious obligation, comes from *mitzaveh*, command. A mitzvah is a commandment of God incumbent upon the Jew. But do you and I believe in a commanding God?

I do not. I have written you about my understanding of God. We shall speak more of it I am sure. So let me add a bit here. Throughout Torah men and women encounter God. These encounters happen in different ways: voices, dreams, angels, a burning bush. From their various encounters they feel compelled to do certain things: to speak certain words, to travel to a certain place, to liberate a people enslaved.

A mitzvah is what we take with us after an encounter with God. It is not that God commands us to do such and such, but rather that our encounter with God compels us to do it. Our encounter with God fills us with godliness and the desire to repair the world, and we go about this in ways that reflect our personality, our history, and our circumstances.

Of course, if this were all there were to mitzvot, there would be very few and they would be anything but communal obligations. So there is more.

Moshe Rabbeinu is our Law Giver. It is from him that most of our mitzvot are derived. It is from his encounters with God that our mitzvot draw their power. Moshe meets God and can no longer see the stranger as "other," so he commands us to love the stranger as we love ourselves. Moshe meets God and can no longer see people as being enslaved by work, so he proclaims the Sabbath, a day of no work when we can reclaim our original stature as divine beings in paradise. Moshe encounters God and can no longer look the other way when sellers steal from buyers with false weights and measures, so he proclaims honest measures and business integrity as the command of God. Moshe meets God and can no longer see the divisions among people, so he challenges us to love our neighbors as ourselves.

Do you understand? I am not saying that each of us must meet God and follow only those mitzvot we take away from our meeting. I am saying that there have been and will continue to be great souls among humankind whose meetings with God will result not in personal mitzvot, but global mitzvot for humanity coming through those whose encounter with God surpasses all tribes and divisions.

But not all mitzvot are of this quality. Moshe proclaims the Sabbath and then worries about those who ignore him, so he says that anyone caught picking up sticks on a Saturday will be put to death. Moshe proclaims that children should honor their parents and then worries about those who do not, so he says that the rebellious son shall be put to death.

Are these mitzvot of the same quality as the others? No. They are not rooted in encounter with God, they do not uphold the principle of l'chayyim, they do not speak from love. On the contrary they are commands rooted in fear, and resulting in violence.

Our obligation is only to the mitzvot of l'chayyim and love. A radical position to hold, I understand. But one that must be spoken loudly and clearly.

I cannot help but hear you wondering just what impact my ideas would have on Judaism if more than just you, my friend, took them seriously. I do not wish to sound immodest, but I wonder if the simple Judaism you and I are exploring is not a perfect fit for your America. A person chooses to be a Jew without parental imposition. A Jew has to make teshuvah for himself by seeing what God asks of him in the moment rather than by returning and conforming to an ancient code of practice and belief. Maybe I should move to America.

I am not serious about moving, but I must tell you it is not so good here. There is the usual violence against us, but it is more a mood I sense among the young. They do not have the faith of their parents and grandparents. They do not trust that this is all part of God's divine plan. We suffer for Him. We die for Him. Interesting— the Christians say their God dies for them; we say we die for God. How sad that the central image of faith is death. No wonder there is a loss of hope among the young; despair is the true enemy of the spirit.

Now I am getting tired. So I will go rest and send this off to you tomorrow.

B'Shalom

SHABBAT AND THE HOLY DAYS

My dearest Aaron Hershel,

Now here is a question dear to my heart! What to do about *Shabbat*. First let me tell you something that you did not say but which maybe you were embarrassed to say. I know that America is not Mogelev. I know that many Jews there no longer live as we Jews do here. So when you ask me about Shabbat, I can only surmise that you are becoming more American and, God forbid, less Jewish.

But, then, what is Jewish? Months and months ago I said to you that Judaism was, at its heart, tikkun and teshuvah. Repairing the world by bringing our attention to each moment and engaging that moment in a godly manner. Am I now going to tell you that there is but one way to do this? There is not. There are many ways, and I rely on the creativity of our people in the new world to find them.

And yet, if Judaism is whatever a person makes of it, it will lack all sense. While I am happy to see many forms of Judaism arise, I am concerned that they are careful to root themselves in a common set of principles. The principles are taught through the form, but it is the principle and not the form that is important to me.

When we talk of Shabbat or any other holy day or mitzvah, then, we must always do three things: First, we must uncover the principle the holy day or mitzvah embodies. Second, we must see if that principle is still true. Third, if it is, we must discover if the old form is the best way for us to live it. If the old form works, then we follow the old way. If it does not work we must create a new form. We cannot afford to lose the principle because the form no longer articulates it. What matters is the principle and not the form, so we can, if necessary, change the form to save the principle.

What is the principle of Shabbat? Rest, certainly, but not only the surface rest like that of taking a nap, but a much deeper rest, a stopping of the past. Let's go into this slowly.

What does Torah tell us about the principle of Shabbat? "Thus the heaven and the earth were finished, and all their array. By the seventh day God completed His work that He had done, and He abstained on the seventh day from all His work which He had done. God blessed the seventh day and sanctified it because on it He abstained from all His work of creation," (Genesis 2:1-3).

Why the constant repetition of "work which He had done"? To teach us that the work that God ceases doing on the Sabbath is the work of the past. God cannot cease to act altogether, for then the world, which is simply God manifest in time and space, would cease to be. The Sabbath puts the past to rest. The Sabbath is only about being present in the present.

You and I spend most of our time in the past. The rest we spend in the future. We are always mulling over what was and worrying about what will be. But not on Shabbat. On Shabbat we let both the past and the future alone, and simply luxuriate in the present. This is the true meaning of Sabbath rest.

What does this rest bring us? Two things.

First it brings an end to our alienation from creation. "Remember the Sabbath day to sanctify it... For in six days God made the heavens and the earth, the sea and all that is in them, and He rested on the seventh day...," (Exodus 20:8). On Shabbat we put an end to all our struggles to create, and remember that creation itself comes from God.

So much of our time is spent wrestling with nature, wresting from her what we need to meet what we think are our real needs. On Shabbat we cease all that work and discover that our true needs are few and simple. We find that our deepest need is the need to belong. This is why we spend so much of Shabbat eating, singing, and delighting in being with others in the world. It is our struggle to make the world go the way we want it to go that alienates us from the world and from others. On Shabbat this struggle stops and the natural friendship of all beings is allowed to flourish.

Second, it brings an end to slavery and the taste of liberation. "Safeguard the Sabbath to sanctify it... and you shall remember that you were slaves in the land of Egypt, and the Lord God took you out from there... therefore the Lord your God commands you to make the Sabbath day," (Deuteronomy 5:12-15).

On Shabbat we remember our enslavement so that we might fully taste what it is to be free. Egypt in Hebrew is *mitzrayim*, the narrow places. It is not simply an ancient civilization but an ever-present state of mind. Throughout the week we are trapped in the narrow places of power and self-focus. We become slaves to those things that promise to set us free. On Shabbat we put all those things aside and discover that we are already free. Freedom is not won, it is affirmed and defended. Keeping Shabbat does both.

So this is the principle underlying Shabbat: the cessation from those acts that enslave us to self and selfishness and thus alienate us from the world of nature and our fellow humans.

In our village we go to shul and pray; we eat festive meals with family and friends; we study; we sing; we go for a stroll; we make love. Do these no longer work for you in America? Do American Jews not eat, or sing, or walk? Have you no time for prayer and study and love? Maybe not. Which is why you need Shabbat all the more!

I know that you may choose to make Shabbat differently than you did living with your family here in Russia. All I ask is that when you choose what form your Shabbat will take you make sure that it embodies the principles for which Shabbat stands.

Now I want to offer something for which you did not ask. If Shabbat and Yontif are about form embodying principle, what are principles of the other holy days?

I want to share these with you and let you work out the forms for yourself. I will be very brief with each, and only comment on the most important holy days. From this you will understand the idea I am presenting to you, and you will then be able to apply it on your own.

Rosh haShanah, the anniversary of creation. The principle? The rootedness of all life in God. All life comes from God and each life carries an obligation to act in a godly way. On Rosh haShanah we look to see where we have been godly and where we have not. We strengthen the first and fix the second.

Yom Kippur, the Day of Atonement. This is a day devoted to teshuvah, returning to our true nature as beings in the image and likeness of God. We turn to God and discover that the distance between us is gone. We find that God's embrace is constant; it is only that we refuse to feel it. On Yom Kippur we allow ourselves to feel our unity with God.

Sukkot is our harvest holy day of thanksgiving. The principles are thanksgiving and transience. We spend the week eating with friends and family in booths *(sukkot)* filled with signs of nature's bounty. We give thanks for the blessings we receive each day, and vow to be a blessing to others. But our booths are open to the elements, reminding us that there is no defense against the impermanence of life. We do not allow life's impermanence to blind us to life's beauty. Impermanence is not the enemy of life, it is the larger context in which life happens, and we are thankful for both.

Hanukkah, the Festival of Lights. What was the real miracle of Hanukkah? That the tiny army of Judah Maccabee chased out the massive army of the Greeks and Syrians from our land? No mean feat, but not a miracle. That the oil needed to rededicate the Temple after the fighting was insufficient to last for the eight days of the rededication ceremony, and yet did just that? A surprise to be sure, but to me the real miracle of Hanukkah is that knowing they did not have enough oil to finish the rededication they chose to start anyway. Where is the logic in this? Logic says: We must wait until we have the resources we need before we reconnect with God. Hanukkah says: Start where you are, the rest will take care of itself.

Purim, the bravery of Queen Esther saving our people from a Persian pogrom. We are to get so drunk on Purim that we cannot tell the difference between Mordecai the Just and Haman the Wicked, may his name be blotted out forever. What does this mean? We must realize that it is not always so clear what is right and what is wrong, but that we cannot let confusion keep us from acting to save lives. On Purim we give *tzedakah* (charity) to everyone. We do not judge, we just give. The principle of Purim is to step beyond judgment and act l'chayyim.

Pesach, our liberation from slavery. We are all enslaved some-where. We all enslave others sometime. Pesach is a week to investigate and put an end to both. *Chametz* (the leavened foods forbidden during Passover) reminds us of the sourness we bring to life through slavery. We avoid it in food to remind us to avoid it in life.

Shavuot, the anniversary of the giving of the Torah at Mount Sinai. Pesach sets us free, but is it just *freedom from* or is it also *freedom for?* Freedom from slavery, yes. Freedom to follow a higher law, also yes. Freedom is not anarchy. And we move into Shavuot seeking the eternal truths we need to uplift the world to godliness.

Is this all there is to our holy days? Of course not. This is a short guide to some of their timeless principles. The principles tell us why we are to observe these holy days. I am certain there are rabbis even in America who will be happy to help with how.

I trust that Judaism will thrive in your hands, my friend.

B'Shalom

ISRAEL

My dearest Aaron Hershel,

Your letters bring such *nachas* to me. You adventures in America are, of course, interesting but it is your resolve to make time for Torah that gives me the most joy. When I hear people cluck their tongues and speak of the end of *Yiddishkeit* in America I always tell them about you. Because of you I have much hope for all our people who seek a new life in that world. So how ironic that with all your success in the new world, you write to me of the ancient world of Israel.

Yet, I must keep this letter short. I am not feeling well. Nothing serious, I trust, but enough to make thinking hard and writing harder. But if I do not respond to you now I am afraid too much time will pass and the rhythm of our conversation will suffer. So, you ask about Israel.

We talked already about who is a Jew and that should have been the same as who comprises the people Israel. But you want to talk about the so-called heresy of Zionism.

Remember Alexander Krupchick? His daughter had the limp. He and his family were Zionists. They moved to Palestine. Shmuel Felder, too. And Rayzl Sitskein. Maybe they will find partners there. Maybe they will find each other there. Stranger things have happened.

I have read a bit about Zionism, and heard a speech or two. What do I think? I don't know enough to have an informed opinion, but what is a rabbi without some opinion? So I will have an opinion and share it with you.

Do I think Jews should rebuild Israel without waiting for *Mashiach* (Messiah)? No and yes. That is a good opinion, don't you think? Now what do I mean?

No, Jews should not return and rebuild Palestine without seeing themselves as embodying the messianic hopes and dreams of our people. The Mashiach is to return us to Israel for what purpose? So that we can be an *or l'goyyim*, a light unto the nations of the world. We are charged with creating the perfect society: justice and compassion for all.

If our Zionist brothers and sisters hope to build a homeland that is without this messianic mission and light, then I would say it is not enough. Yes, I understand that if we had our own land we could leave the pogroms behind. And I would be the last person to discount the good in that idea. Yet, I would argue, assuming anyone would bother to ask, that a Jewish state without the messianic spark in the hearts of its people and the messianic challenge at the heart of its government would be no less a diaspora from what we Jews are supposed to be than any small village in Russia. So that is my opinion "no."

Now to my opinion "yes." Yes, they should not wait for a messiah to come from among us and work magic. We have had such messiahs before, and we rejected them all. Remember Yemen in the days of the Rambam (Rabbi Moses ben Maimon, 10th century)? They had a messiah. They wrote to Rambam and asked him how they could know if this was THE messiah. He suggested that the fellow do some miracle. He agreed to cut off his head with a sword and then pick it up and replace it on his neck good as new. And he almost succeeded.

And Rabbi Akiva, may his memory be for a blessing, did he not have his messiah, Bar Kochbah? And did not the Jews of Turkey follow the false messiah Shabbatai Tzvi? We have had and will continue to have messiahs. The question is which, if any, are real?

The one who succeeds, that one is real. The one who gathers up our people, leads them home to Jerusalem, helps them create a government that is indeed an or l'goyyim, and opens the hearts of our people to God. This one I will call Mashiach.

So let us see if Mashiach is among the Zionists. If they do what our messianic hope asks of them, then there was no need to wait for a messiah, they were Mashiach themselves. The proof is in the product.

So I say this: let them reclaim and rebuild our homeland. If at least they make a sanctuary for us Jews, they should be praised. If at most they pave the way for the redemption of the world, who is to criticize? I wish them and you well, my son. And do not think you need keep your own feelings a secret. I can tell from your letter you think of yourself as a Zionist. I am proud of you.

B'Shalom

INTERMARRIAGE

My dearest Aaron Hershel,

Your latest question took me completely by surprise. What do I think about a marriage between a Jew and Gentile? I don't know what prompted you to ask this question, but your timing is uncanny. Just this week Rochel Miriam, the baker's daughter, ran off to marry a Christian. What a *shanda* (scandal)! Her parents came to me to help set up the *shivah* (a period of mourning; when a Jewish child converts, the parents are to act as if she has died). Rabbi Levi ben Joseph was out of town, so it fell to me. Tell me, what should I have done? What would you do? Tradition is tradition. And yet I could not do it.

I sat them down and said: "Two men are wandering lost in the woods. Neither has any idea how to get home. In time they come to a fork in the path they are taking. One goes east, the other west. What they do not know is that both roads lead them home. Soon they have walked far enough apart that the one is no longer visible to the other. Suddenly the man on the eastward road starts to wail. 'My friend is dead,' he cries, 'my friend is dead.' Does this make sense to you?"

Shlomo the baker's face was hard as a three-day old bagel. He said: "No, the friend is not dead, only on a different path. And in time both will meet each other at the trails' end." His wife sobbed quietly.

"So?" I said.

"So?" Shlomo said. "What do these crazy wanderers have to do with us and our daughter?"

And then his wife, Chana says to him in a cracked and weary voice: "The three of us are the wanderers, Shlomo. Rochel is on one path and we are on the other. Should we mourn for her, and pretend she is dead, or should we wait for her to finish her path and meet us at home?"

Shlomo stared at me.

"Shlomo," I said. "I cannot help you sit shivah for a daughter who is not dead. Nor can I believe that God is so narrow that only one path leads to Him. God is not Jewish or Christian or Moslem. God is God. It is we who imagine different gods at the end of different paths. But we shall see when we arrive that there is only the One."

Shlomo said: "So?" His voice was barely audible.

"So," I said, "Go home with your wife, and send a letter to your daughter telling her that you will always be her parents and she your daughter, and that your door is always open to her, her husband, and, God willing, her children."

"And when our friends ask us what happened, what do we say then?"

"Tell them that your daughter is happy. That she is a good woman who has married a good man and together they will raise good children. Tell them God is happy for her as well, for God needs good people to find each other and raise good families. The world needs more good people."

"And when we hear them mocking us behind our backs?"

"Then you will know they are not your friends. Some will mock you. But others will sigh with relief that someone finally had the courage to end a custom that comes not from God but just the fearful hearts of frightened parents and their rabbis."

So do you know what happened, my dear Aaron Hershel? Shlomo and Chana went home and did not cover a single mirror for two days. (It is customary to cover mirrors during shivah). Then Reb Levi returned and declared that the entire town sit shivah for a week!

It can get pretty lonely here, Hershele. And pretty late. God bless you.

B'Shalom

WHY BE JEWISH?

My dearest Aaron Hershel,

Your last letter took me by surprise! But then I realized that maybe my liberal thinking on Jews who marry Gentiles sparked the question. I tried to think when I have been asked such a question before, and I think this may be the first time. "Why be Jewish?" For a moment I did not even understand what you were asking me. But as I read on I discovered the reason behind your question.

You know, I don't think our Gentile neighbors ever ask us why we are Jews. Our Jewishness is a given; they either hate us, or tolerate us, or ignore us or treat us as equals. But has any one of them ever inquired about us? This would be a rare person indeed. But America is not Russia, is it? America is something unique. People are curious about each other. Perhaps because Americans are free to choose which religion to follow, they are curious about all of them and why one person makes one choice and another person makes a different choice.

Why be Jewish? It seems to me that there are two people who would ask this question. There is the Jew who is thinking about leaving Judaism, and there is the Gentile who is thinking about adopting it. My answer to both would be the same: Be a Jew because being a Jew is the best way for you to fulfill your potential as a human being created in the image of God. I imagine that they would then ask me: But how do I know what my potential as a human being is? And how do I know if being a Jew would help me achieve this potential?

No one knows what her potential is. No one knows how far he can go or how high she can reach. What seems to be your limit today proves to be but a stepping-stone tomorrow. Perhaps the only way to know what we can achieve in life is to look back from our deathbeds and see just what we did achieve. You could argue that this does not make sense: Could I not have made different choices in my life? Could I have not taken a different path and achieved more than I did?

To my mind, the answer is no. If you could have lived differently you would have lived differently. You lived the way you lived because that was all you could do. Comparing it to what you imagine you could have done is an unfair comparison. Why did I choose to be a rabbi? Could I have chosen otherwise? Do not imagine that at a certain age someone came to me and laid out all the possible things a person can be and said to me: Now choose. No one gave me such a clear choice, and no one decision brought me to the rabbinate. Rather, thousands of little decisions carried me here. I was drawn to study and not farming. I was captivated by the talmudic sages and not musicians. Why? Could I go back and back into my life and discover a straight line of cause and effect leading to this very moment?

What you would find is that each choice builds upon those that preceded it. No choice happens in a completely free space. I am a rabbi because after making thousands of little choices that seemed to have nothing to do with being a rabbi it became impossible for me to be anything else.

We are not free to be anyone we wish. We are free only to be who we are. And real freedom lies in knowing that, and in taking up your destiny as it reveals itself to you. So how do we know what our potential is? We do not know in advance. We only know what choice seems right to us at the moment. Then another choice appears and we must choose rightly once again; and then again and again and again until we discover a pattern to our choosing. This pattern is our destiny. At first we may create it. In the end it creates us.

If this is so, then how can anyone know if being or becoming a Jew is right for them? If they stand back and try to be objective, they will never know. The only way to know is to make a choice and see.

If a Gentile were to come to me and inquire about becoming a Jew, what would I say? I would say: "Live as a Jew for one year. Keep *kashrut*, make Shabbat, observe the Holy Days, study Torah. Then, at the end of a year, you will know for yourself if this is the choice you are to make."

What would I say to a Jew who comes to see if she should remain a Jew? If she knows nothing about being a Jew, I would make the same suggestion as I make to a Gentile: try it and see. If she is a knowledgeable Jew, an observant Jew, then I would say this: find a path that works for you.

We have spoken months ago about the purpose of being human. Our task is to till the soil of self to let it breathe the life-giving air of the soul. We must talk about soul some day, but for now let me simply say that if Judaism does not till your soil you must find another way that does. God never commands us to be Jewish, God commands us to be holy (Leviticus 19:2). To be holy means to make the world holy. You can do this only if you are in touch with your deepest divine nature.

Why be Jewish? Because being Jewish is the most powerful way to break open the ego and experience God. If there is a better way for you to follow, then follow it.

I am to travel far from our village tomorrow. A dear friend is dying. I will stay until the death and through the shivah. Write when you can. I will answer when I return.

B'Shalom

SOUL

My dearest Aaron Hershel,

Am I so old that we should speak of souls and death? I will assume you are simply curious and in no hurry for me to check out the accuracy of what I teach.

Your thoughts on the nature of the human soul were most interesting. You grasped the problem immediately: If the soul is a permanent self that lives forever then the entire nature of God is undone!

God is both Yesh and Ayn, the transient and the timeless. Only the former imagines separate selves or souls. The latter knows only oneness. Eternal life in the world to come is a concept arising from the desire of the seeming separate self, the Neshamah, to deny its eventual and inevitable dissolution in death. It is fear of death that leads us to imagine separate souls and an after-life. In truth there is none of this. The conventional notion of soul as eternal self is simply the Neshamah's sense of separateness projected into a never-ending future.

The sad thing is that with all our efforts to bolster what is ultimately a false sense of self and eternity, we miss the real immortality of which we are a part. Ayn, that aspect of reality that is empty of self and separateness, is deathless, birthless, selfless, and timeless. And we humans are no less Ayn than Yesh.

The individual human being is like a wave on an ocean. From the surface each wave appears unique, independent, and transient. Yet beneath the surface all waves are one, interdependent, and eternal. From the perspective of the surface, each wave is born, runs its course, and dies. From the deeper perspective of the ocean there is no birth, no separate life, no death.

It is the same with people. On the surface, from the perspective of Yesh, we appear to be born, live, and die. But beneath the surface, from the perspective of Ayn, we find that there is no separate self and thus no birth, no destiny, no death. Insofar as we tap what is beneath the surface we are calm, compassionate, and just. Insofar as we focus only on the surface we are anxious, violent, and frightened.

Rather than define soul as an essential and deathless self, which we know to be false, we should understand soul as human consciousness. According to our sages there are five dimensions to human consciousness, each one larger and more inclusive that the ones before it.

The first and least inclusive is *Nefesh* or life force, which is the level of soul that operates according to the dictates of nature. It is Nefesh that tells your heart to beat and your lungs to breath. The second is *Ruach*, instinct, and is the level of soul that operates to ensure your survival as a living being. It is Ruach that tells you to duck when a stone flies by your head.

Ruach and Nefesh are unconscious in that they operate without a fully developed sense of separate self. A fully self-conscious self arises with the third level of soul, *Neshamah*, ego. It is Neshamah that says *I, me,* and *mine*. It is Neshamah that insists it is separate and self-contained. It is Neshamah that imagines that it can live without the body, and thus survive death.

The fourth level of soul is *Chayyah*, cosmic consciousness, the level of consciousness that is aware of the interconnectedness of all things as Ayn. Chayyah still has a sense of self, but it does not see itself as separate from other selves. Chayyah sees itself as a knot in an infinitely knotted net, unique and yet at one with all other knots. Chayyah knows itself as part of God but does not yet see itself as God.

The fifth level of soul is *Yechidah*, unity consciousness. Here there is no Yesh or Ayn, just a pure contentless knowing without knower or known. Yechidah is completely at one with God. When the great kabbalist Abraham Abulafia (1240 - 1291) proclaimed at the height of mystic revelry: "*Ani hu!* I am He," he was speaking from the perspective of Yechidah where everything is known as a manifestation of the one thing, God.

These five levels of soul correspond to five dimensions of reality, each dimension larger than and inclusive of the ones before it. This is what our kabbalists call the Five Worlds.

Nefesh consciousness knows the world as *Assiyah*, the blind doings of nature. Ruach consciousness knows the world as Yetzirah, the instinctual world of animals that have not yet reached reflective self-consciousness. Neshamah consciousness knows the world as *Beriah*, the world of creative, self-aware, and reflective beings, especially human beings. Chayyah consciousness knows the world as *Atzilut*, the world of divine emanation where all forms are seen and honored as aspects of God. Yechidah consciousness knows the world as *Adam Kadmon*, primordial reality, pure spirit, formless emptiness.

All five levels of consciousness and all five dimensions of reality are present in each of us at all times. We tend to focus on the self-conscious Neshamah and the Beriah world of competing selves, and to ignore all other realms and means of knowing, unless something goes wrong. For example:

We become aware of Assiyah and Nefesh when there is something wrong with us physically. A broken leg demands we focus on Assiyah, and pulls us away from other modes of knowing to concentrate and deal with our pain.

We become aware of Yetzirah and Ruach when we are confronted with unexpected danger. We are suddenly face to face with a bear and our minds and bodies react—we run away. There is no need for self-reflection. Ruach tells Nefesh to run and our legs run!

We become aware of Beriah and Neshamah every time we say *I*, *me*, and *mine*. This is the world that occupies most of our attention. It is the world in which we feel most at home. It is also the world from which most of our suffering comes.

We become aware of Atzilut and Chayyah when we sleep, or when we are deep in prayer or selfless meditation, or when we are blessed with a sudden insight or intuition that comes from beyond our ordinary ability to know. Both sleep and meditation quiet Neshamah's incessant *I'ing* and we are exposed to a more inclusive reality. Intuition happens only when Neshamah is quiet, for only then can intuition be heard above the din of Beriah.

We "become aware" of Adam Kadmon and Yechidah when we are aware of nothing at all. This is the paradox of Yechidah consciousness: it is that aspect of ourselves that realizes there are no selves. You do not know you are Yechidah conscious because there is no you to know in Adam Kadmon. Only when you return to Chayyah or Neshamah from an awakening of Yechidah can you sense the experience. You feel lighter, more joyous, at peace with self and other, and filled with compassion for everyone and everything.

So let's return to our wave and ocean analogy and see if we can put all this business about soul into some clear form. Imagine yourself to be a wave in the ocean. Assiyah is the raw stuff of the ocean, and the laws that dictate its nature and capacity to wave are the doings of Nefesh. Without Nefesh you could not emerge from the ocean, but you do not identify yourself with this. Nefesh is preconscious.

Yetzirah is the world of currents and surf, the laws that govern the shapes of waves and their duration in time are the workings of Ruach consciousness. These too are preconscious, for while they are essential to your coming into form, you do not usually think of them when you become aware of your form.

Beriah is the dimension of separate waves. Each wave is unique, and recognizing uniqueness is the work of Neshamah consciousness. This is what we call normal consciousness.

Atzilut is the ocean. The ocean creates an infinite number of waves, but it is always the same ocean. When we use our Chayyah consciousness we know this to be so. If Nefesh and Ruach are preconscious, that is, below the awareness of Neshamah, Chayyah is transconscious, including Neshamah in a larger reality.

Adam Kadmon is the essence of the ocean, the very wetness of water itself. When we tap into Yechidah consciousness we know the ocean as it knows itself, not as surface or deep, but simply as wetness. Here all the distinctions of Nefesh, Ruach, Neshamah, and Chayyah merge into an ineffable oneness. I cannot even say it is one for that implies two. I cannot say it is the One for that implies the Many. Adam Kadmon is neither one or many, it is simply nondual. Nondual simply means that there is only one thing and all things are manifestations of it. All waves are a manifestation of the one ocean; all creation is a manifestation of the One God.

So what are you to take with you from all of this? Three things. First, you are not what you think you are. The you that thinks, the Neshamah, is only part of who you are. Second, the extent to which you insist that the you Neshamah says you are is the only you there is is the extent to which you are alienated from God, from nature, and from other beings, for alienation is at the heart of what it is to see the world through Neshmah's eyes. Third, you are also and already Chayyah and Yechidah consciousness. You already know that you are one with the One, and intuit in a nonverbal way that you are nothing but the One.

What is left for you to learn is how to till the hard-packed self of Neshamah and let in the life giving breath of Chayyah and Yechidah That is a conversation for another time. For now it is time for the evening prayers.

B'Shalom

WALKING INWARD

My dearest Aaron Hershel,

I left the door open for you to ask me about how we till the soil of Neshamah to let in the life that is Chayyah and Yechidah, and your insight regarding the idea of spiritual practice was quite interesting. You understand that God's shlemut, God's unity, means that God is right here and now: in you, with you, as you. Neshamah is no less of God than Chayyah and Yechidah. The difference is that it pretends to be other than God, and that pretending is so strong that we begin to act as if it were so. In truth, there can be no separation from God. We have spoken of this in the context of Rabbi Luria. He imagined a world where God is other and broken, and our task is to repair God to wholeness. But it is not God who is broken; it is we who are broken. It is not God who is other than us; it is we who insist upon being other than God.

Who does all this insisting? Neshamah, the self that imagines it is all we are. The result of all spiritual practice is to open the Neshamah to the greater reality of God in which it resides. This is what I mean when I speak of Neshamah opening to Chayyah. This is like a wave realizing it is part of the ocean. It discovers its true nature, its true home. And in so doing it becomes more compassionate, more loving.

But how? How are we to open to the greater reality of God in, with, and as all things? Torah provides us with the answer when it tells of God's call to Avram: *Lech lecha!* Lech lecha means, literally, walk (*lech*) into your self (*lecha*). What self? Not Neshamah, but Chayyah. How? Read the rest of the command: "*Lech lecha!* Get yourself out of your land, away from your relatives, out of your father's house to a land that I will show you," (Genesis 12:1).

To walk into yourself is to see the "land" God wishes us to see. Not a literal land of rock and dirt, but a holy land of milk and honey; a spiritual land that nurtures and enlivens. How do you get there? By freeing yourself from your culture, your tribe, and your parents.

I went to get water from the well last evening, and left the bucket of water outside to stay cool. When I went to drink from the bucket this morning I found a thin layer of ice had formed on the surface of the water. I had to crack the surface ice to drink the water. Now it is true that both the solid ice and the liquid water are the same; they are both water in different forms. Why did I not drink the ice? Because ice does not meet my need for a glass of water. For that I need liquid. So I broke through the one to reach the other. It is the same with spiritual practice.

All is God. Neshamah, the hardened ego, and Chayyah the compassionate soul, are both of God. Neshamah is like ice and Chayyah is like water, and only the latter can slake my spiritual thirst. So I have to crack the ice of Neshamah and drink the water of Chayyah. Spiritual practice is how I crack the ice.

Do not think the ice is bad or that the ice is your enemy. I have said that Neshamah is a necessary part of you; without it you could not run your business or care for a wife and family. But with Neshamah alone you will do these things without the deepest joy and compassion of which you are capable. For that you need Chayyah. And for Chayyah you need spiritual practice.

How does Neshamah become hardened? It is trained to be that way by our parents, our relatives, and our culture. Each of these carries with it assumptions about life, rules about living, and biases about others that harden the self. I don't know if this can be avoided. I do know it can be overcome. The ice can be cracked, the water can be sipped, and the self can be softened by the greater truth of the soul. The softening of the self is what I call entering the Promised Land.

I worry that you may not truly understand me here. I worry that you imagine I am saying you must violently wrest yourself free from your people and your past. I am not saying that. God said to Avram: lech lecha, walk inward. Walking is God's command. Don't run, don't flee, don't attack; just walk. Walk gently and purposefully. Walk consciously and continually. Walk inward, not away. And in so doing you will find that place of peace that is the land God wishes each of us to find.

Now I want to talk with you about how to do this walking, but I find myself tiring easily and needing to go to bed earlier than even a few months ago. I trust this will pass, but for now I must rest. I will send this letter as it is. Think about how you have been hardened and what walking inward toward freedom might mean for you. Then write to me, and if you wish to know how I walk inward, ask and I will share this with you.

B'Shalom

To Listen and to Love

My dearest Aaron Hershel,

Thank you for inquiring after my health. I am simply aging, I suppose. The tiredness is part of the process. I had hoped it would pass, but if anything I am getting weaker rather than stronger. But not too weak to write to you, my friend.

It is quite clear to me that my last letter ended where it should have begun: what are you to do if you wish to walk inward? Maybe I am beginning to ramble in my old age. Or maybe I am just not so eager to tell you everything and risk the end of our conversation. Nevertheless, what indeed are you to do to walk inward?

What I am about to share with you is so simple, so commonplace, and so much a part of your upbringing as a Jew that you will be surprised that it forms the heart of this inward walking. Several times each day you recite the *Sh'ma*, the central affirmation of our tradition: *Sh'ma Yisrael, Adonai Eloheinu, Adonai Echad:* Hear, O Israel, the One Who Is All Is God, This One Is One (Deuteronomy 6:4). You then continue with the following: "And you shall love the One Who Is All with all your heart, with every breath, with all you have. And these things that I command you today shall be upon your heart. You shall teach them carefully to your children; you shall speak of them when you sit at home, when you walk on the road, when you lie down, and when you rise up. Bind them on your hand, keep them before your eyes. Write them on the doorposts of your homes and on your gates" (Deuteronomy 6:5-9).

Can you see in this paragraph of Torah the secret to lech lecha? Can you see here what you are to do to till the soil of Neshamah and allow it to breathe the breath of Chayyah? It is simple: to listen and to love. This is the core of my spiritual practice: I listen and I love.

Of course I can almost hear your confusion: What about Shabbat, kashrut, the Holy Days? These are dear to my heart and part of my life, but they are not the key to the inward walking that we spoke about last time. We both know people whose Neshamah is hard as ice and yet who carefully observe the Sabbath. To move inward from Neshamah to Chayyah we need a special practice, and this passage of Torah reveals it to us. Let me explain.

First, what does it mean to listen? When a loved one asks to speak with you about something important, something precious to her, how do you listen? With your whole being. You turn away from distractions. You focus your attention. You quiet the chatter in your own mind in order to make room for the concerns of another's mind. This is true listening. And more: When you listen in this way you do so without any idea of what you will hear or how you will respond.

This is important to realize, my dear Hershele. If you already know what you will say to the other, there is no need to listen. All you need do is wait for an opening so you can say what you intended to say regardless of what the other is saying to you. This is not listening. When you listen you do so without preconceptions. Do you see how this connects to our earlier discussion of lech lecha? You are to move inward and free yourself from what you know in order to respond freely to what the other is saying.

So listening requires self-emptying, the quieting of the Neshamah. I will tell you how to do this in a moment. First let me continue with my thoughts of the text itself.

Who is the Israel addressed here? Is it just the Jews? I do not think so. Torah is given through the Jews to the world, and must address more than our people alone. *Yisrael* means one who struggles with the divine—*yisra El.* And that can mean people of any religion and none. So the Torah is speaking to all who seek God and says to them: Listen!

And if you listen, what will you hear? The unity of God as All in All. This is what is meant by "God is One." Not that God is singular rather than plural; but that there is only one reality and that reality is God.

Listening, then, reveals the absolute shlemut of God. But now what? Can you stay in that place of listening, which is Chayyah? Can you stay in Chayyah and not return to Neshamah? On the contrary, when you truly hear, realize, and know that God is all in All, you naturally return to the world of Beriah, the world of competing Neshamahs because this too is God. Hearing the oneness of God returns you to the world of Beriah, the everyday reality of seemingly separate things, and the Neshamah consciousness that accompanies it. You know that all is God, even Neshamah, so there is no need to reject anything, especially Neshamah. So you return, but you return changed.

Here is how you are changed: The Sh'ma is followed by the next sentence, v'ahavta, "and you shall love." We are used to reading this as a command: You must love, but how can God demand love? Love is a feeling and feelings are uncontrollable by the will. They come and they go, and there is not much we can do about them. Demanding that we feel one way all the time is to ask of us the impossible.

So what is the meaning of "You shall love"? It isn't a command, it is a consequence. Do not read "You must love"; read "You will love." In other words, if you listen and hear the unity of God as all reality, then you will love God as all reality and all reality as God.

This is the transformation of Neshamah. This is what happens when Neshamah is tilled by spiritual practice: You engage the world with love.

You feel the unity of God in your heart. You teach your children and all children the nature of this love. You speak of it when sitting, walking, lying down, and getting up. These are the four basic postures of any human being, meaning that this love will shape all of your doing in the world. The doings of your hands will reflect the quality of your listening by expressing the depth of your loving. Your face will radiate love as a jewel radiates light. And then there is this business about the doorposts and gates. So wonderful!

What are the doorposts? The pillars that allow you to enter from one room to another in your home. Each is to be marked in a way that reminds you to listen and to love. This is the purpose of placing a *mezzuzah* on each doorway of those rooms in which you live. Think of this: Place a mezzuzah on the doorpost of the kitchen and make sure that love is the main ingredient in the food you cook. Place one on the bedroom doorpost and remember that true intimacy comes from listening. Each room has its sacredness; honor it with listening and loving, and help remind yourself to do so by placing a mezzuzah on its doorpost.

And what of the gates? The gates are where you meet the rest of the world. You home is for intimates and friends, the gates are for strangers. Only once does Torah say, "Love your neighbor" (Leviticus 19:18), but "Love the stranger" Torah says dozens of times! (for example, Leviticus 19:34). It is not so difficult to love those close to us, but our natural reaction to the stranger is fear. Torah challenges us to replace fear with love, and to remember to do so you must imagine each encounter as a gateway to love and place a mezzuzah on that moment to remember to listen and love.

I hope you are following me in this, Hershele. It is so important that you see what this inward walking can do. And now let me explain how to do it. The point is to listen. To listen you must be comfortable and quiet. Find a comfortable place to sit. Do not cross your legs or your arms, but sit upright with your feet flat on the floor and your hands resting palms down on your thighs. Close your eyes. Breathe at whatever rhythm your body needs to breathe. Don't move. Now listen.

What do you hear? All kinds of noise, I am certain. This is not a problem. The problem arises if you allow yourself to become distracted by the noise. Here is how to avoid that distraction.

As you breathe in, say to yourself *Sh'ma*. As you breathe out, say to yourself *Yisrael*. Breathe in *Adonai;* breathe out *Eloheinu;* breathe in *Adonai;* breathe out *Echad*.

That is all there is to it. Breathe and recite the Sh'ma. Slowly you will center into a quiet place where the noises within and without do not capture your attention. In time you will find that the space between inhalation and exhalation lengthens. You are not holding your breath, but you simply have less of a need to breathe. Your breathing slows and softens, and with it your mind does the same. When you reach this place there is no need to recite the Sh'ma. Just breathe and listen. Just listen and love.

If your mind wanders, return to the recitation of the Sh'ma. When you are quiet again, be silent.

There is a wonderful teaching in Psalms that captures the essence of this practice: "Be still and know I am God" (Psalm 46:10). To be still is to listen, to listen is to know, to know is to love. Do this twice a day for at least half an hour each time and you will find your Neshamah softened by Chayyah and your life transformed by listening and love.

B'Shalom

IS IT WORKING?

My dearest Aaron Hershel,

So I send off this long letter of instruction and I get back this short query: "How do I know it is working?" Oy, I wonder about that sometimes myself. This is what I have discovered.

First, let me say that you should not enter into these practices with a goal in mind. They should be done *lishma*, for their own sake. Why is this so? Because it is Neshamah that sets goals, and the goal it sets for spiritual practice is its own transcendence. This cannot be done! Neshamah cannot transcend itself any more than your teeth can bite themselves. Unlike your teeth, though, Neshamah can fool itself into thinking it has done so.

There is a self-anointed *tzaddik* in our village, Reb Tzvi Hirsch haCohen. He is convinced and goes to great lengths to convince others that he is a great spiritual teacher, a man who has set aside Neshamah altogether and resides only in the just and compassionate space of Chayyah. Nu, maybe he is right? How can I judge?

I will tell you. I judge his claims by the quality of his actions. Is he kind, just, merciful, compassionate? Is he more of these than the rest of us? Not only is the second not true, I doubt even the truth of the first. He is so full of himself as to leave no room for the needs of others. This is not a person who has set Neshamah in the greater compassion of Chayyah. This is simply a selfish person masquerading as a selfless one.

And, sad to say, many fall for his act. So many of us are hungry for an authentic teacher of inward walking that we mistake every charlatan for a saint. Reb Tzvi is loud, energetic, and filled with words that fly by so fast few of his listeners notice that they make no sense. His knowledge is vast but his wisdom is shallow. Worse still, his actions stem from Neshamah not Chayyah.

In my understanding, we know we are truly listening because our lives are more loving. But it is important that we understand what being loving is in this context. We learn this from the Thirteen Attributes of Godliness.

Moses asks God to show him His face. God says no one can see His face and live. Why? Because God's face includes your face and the faces of all things. Just as your pointer finger cannot point to itself, or your ears hear themselves, or your nose smell itself, you cannot see God's face.

Yet God says He will shield Moses in a cleft of a rock and pass by allowing Moses to experience what we might call the wake of God. You might not see a ship passing, but you can see the impact of its presence on the water. What is God's wake? What is the impact of God's presence? The Thirteen Attributes that Moses hears as God passes by.

The first three of these are ineffable. Torah simply lists them as "The One Who Is All; The One Who Is All; God," but the remaining nine are understandable: compassionate, graceful, patient, abundantly kind, abundantly honest, preserving of kindness, forgiving iniquity, forgiving willfulness, forgiving error, cleanser of stains and grudges (Exodus 34:5-7).

When you listen to the unity of God as all in All you engage the world with love. Engaging the world with love means that you live these attributes of God. You are compassionate, graceful, patient, kind, and truthful. You remember the good people do. You forgive their mistakes over and over again, and you do not hold their past against them.

If you wish to know if you are walking inwardly; if you wish to know if you are truly listening to the One Who Is All, look to the quality of your actions. Are you becoming more compassionate, patient, kind, and the rest? If so, then you are listening and loving. If not, then you are not.

The process of inquiring after these attributes is called *cheshbon hanefesh,* an accounting of the soul. Each evening before going to sleep ask yourself, for example: Just how compassionate am I? Review situations during the day when you acted with compassion and times when you did not. Can you see why you were compassionate in one instance and not in another? Pay attention and become aware when compassion is present or when it should be called upon. Work honestly with yourself to identify compassion and when to use it. You will know when you are doing it right because you will sense a bond, a union, between you and the person you are engaging. This is tikkun, the repairing of your seemingly separate self in the greater unity of God.

When you feel you have taken compassion as far as you can, take up grace. And then each attribute in turn until you feel you have studied them all. And when you have done them all? Start again. There is no end to consciously cultivating the attributes of God.

I imagine you reading this at night. So now go to sleep. And before you do, ask yourself a few questions.

B'Shalom

RELIGION

My dearest Aaron Hershel,

I am pleased that your business goes well, and somewhat envious of your travels. You observe many different religious people on your trade journeys and you wonder what is the purpose of religion. I will do my best to explain.

There are people among us who have the ability to set Neshamah aside and perceive the world from the perspectives of Chayyah and Yechidah. These are the prophets and great sages that have arisen in every age among every people. Since most of us cannot attain these prophetic heights we create a system to preserve the teachings of those who do. Religion is that system.

There is a game the children play where one child whispers a message into the ear of a second child who in turn whispers it to a third and on and on until the last child speaks aloud what has been passed on. This received message is then compared to the original message and the distortion of the first to the last sends the children into gales of laughter. This game can teach us a lot about religion.

What does the *Pirke Avot (The Sayings of the Fathers)* say? "Moshe received the Torah from God on Mount Sinai. He in turn passed it on to Joshua who passed it on to the Prophets who passed it on to the Men of the Great Assembly," *(Pirke Avot* 1:1). Is this not the same game? Does it not lend itself to the same problem of distortion?

Of course, I know that our sages deny this, and claim that the word received by Moshe is in fact the word read each week in *shul* (synagogue), but what else can they say? Imagine our rabbis saying to the Jews: "Our message to you is a distortion of God's Word, but it is all we have to go on, so let's do the best we can with it." Where would their authority be then? Who would listen to them?

I once met a Muslim who told me that his bible, the Koran, was the only ancient revelation that had not become distorted in its passing from one generation to the next. The Torah and the Gospels of the Christians were once revelations from God, he explained to me, but over centuries of transmission they have become corrupted. Only the Koran has escaped this fate.

I never debate things such as this, but I could not help thinking to myself: What else could he believe? If Moslems did not have faith in the accuracy of their Koran they would not be Moslems. If Christians did not have faith in the accuracy of their Gospels they would not be Christians. And if we Jews did not have faith in the accuracy of Torah we would not be Jews. But just because our social solidarity demands belief in the accuracy of our respective scriptures, this does not make them accurate.

If a group of children cannot maintain the integrity of a message over the course of a few minutes, can we really expect the integrity of the Torah—or the Gospels or the Koran—to be maintained while passing through hundreds of hands over hundreds of years?

No. Scriptures of all types contain fragments of revelation and great chunks of accumulated misunderstanding. The proper study of scripture is to separate the one from the other. Loyalty to scripture should be a loyalty to the truth and not to the distortions. The problem with religion is that it is often incapable of telling the one from the other.

Imagine our group of children at play. The first child provides the original message to the second and then is called home by her mother. By the time the message reaches the end of the line of children there is no way to know how distorted the message has become because the creator of the original message is gone. All the children can do is argue over which version contains the least amount of distortion.

This is the problem religion must deal with. Moshe received the Torah from God on Sinai. Moshe then passes it on to Joshua. Moshe then dies. Now how is Joshua to know if he is passing on the message as intended? While Moshe lived he could correct any errors that Joshua may make in delivering the message, but after his death there is no way to know for certain what is from God and what is from Joshua.

I imagine you must be thinking that I am about to condemn religion. God forbid! I love my religion and believe it is a repository of great wisdom. But I am not afraid to admit that it also contains great distortion. The question is how do we distinguish between the two?

It is not as difficult as it may seem. The truth is universal or it is not true. The principle upon which all religious truth rests is l'chayyim. Teachings that honor life and hold it precious are true, those that denigrate life are false. Teachings that free human beings to find God for themselves are true, those that enslave people to tradition are false. Teachings that celebrate the unity-through-diversity that is the presence of God in the world of Beriah are true, teachings that seek to reduce nature's vitality and humankind's creativity by enforcing conformity in thought, word, and deed are false.

The history of religion, all religion, is the history of the struggle between these two types of faith: the one that liberates and the one that enslaves. This is the struggle, if you will, between the prophets and the priests. I believe that there are people among us who have the ability to move from the world of Beriah, of separate competing selves, nationalities, ethnicities, and religion, to the worlds of Atzilut and Adam Kadmon where all differences are seen as part of the diversity of God's greater unity, and the truth at its purest. They experience that unity and then return to Beriah filled with it. As they read their respective sacred scriptures and examine the traditions that inform the lives of their respective peoples they make corrections, changes in our understanding and our practice. These changes and corrections bring their scriptures, traditions, religions and people into better alignment with the original message. These people are our prophets, our great sages, our holiest rebbes, and they exist among every people in every age.

What is the message with which these prophets reconnect? While the nuances are unique to each one's community and circumstance, the principle of all of them is the same: l'chayyim. The corrections they teach bring people into alignment with the ultimate truth of one God, one world, one humanity, and one moral code—justice and compassion for all beings. Their message honors not only the particular people and tradition to whom they speak, but the global community of men and women to whom the one God speaks through the many voices of faith.

Religion is too important a part of human life, however, to be left solely to the workings of these prophets. We, too, must struggle to free ourselves and our faith from the falsehood that accrues to it. Through our personal practice of inward walking, of freeing ourselves from attachments to culture, tribe, and family we, too, enter into the promised land of Atzilut and Adam Kadmon and correct for ourselves not only the distortions of our faith but the distortions of our lives. When we move beyond the Neshamah and access the higher more inclusive wisdom of Chayyah and Yechidah we broaden our perspective and can free ourselves from mitzrayim, the narrow places of prejudice and fear that too often shape our lives under the guise of religion and nationality.

While you and I may not be prophets, Hershele, we are capable of tapping the greater truth of God's shlemut and seeing for ourselves what is true. And we can tell the difference between truth and falsehood in faith. If the teaching promotes peace, justice, and compassion among humans and between humans and nature it is true; if it promotes violence, division, and exploitation it is false.

So, what is the purpose of religion? The purpose of religion is to preserve the original teachings of those great saints and sages who tap the higher worlds of Atzilut and Adam Kadmon. What is the problem with religion? The problem with religion is that once these prophets die the religion falls into the hands of priests and religious professionals (yes, even rabbis!) whose loyalty is to their own status and power, rather than to the truth. Periodically new prophets appear seeking to correct the distortions, but they are often resisted by these powerful professionals. If they succeed in driving the prophets away, the religion becomes totally corrupt. If the prophets are allowed to correct the distortions, the religion continues to carry truth from generation to generation.

Given all this, truly religious people should say of their respective faiths: "We know this is not the pristine message, but we believe it points the way toward it. Let us study this pointer and seek to fathom that to which it points." This they should say. What do they say? "These are the words of the living God given to the Elect. If you would find redemption you must follow us. All others are damned."

Such arrogance!

B'Shalom

ARE ALL RELIGIONS TRUE?

My dearest Aaron Hershel,

It has been some time since I last wrote. I was visiting the family of my dear friend Reb Micah. His death was expected, he had been ill for many months, but expected or not the loss and the grief is strongly felt. How sad the loss of a friend can be, but how tragic to watch what has happened to his legacy.

The man had many students. At his death each vied to take his place. Yes, he should have chosen a successor before he died, but he did not. And now it is war. Over what? Over truth? Over holiness? No, these are free to anyone who wishes them. The war is over power and prestige. And the irony is that my sainted friend never saw himself as powerful or famous. He was a simple rabbi, teaching Torah as best he could.

Perhaps I am lucky to have so few students. And luckier still that my best lives thousands of miles away so that he cannot fall prey to illusions of grandeur that haunt the mind of so many so-called religious folk.

But this has nothing to do with your question, if it really is your question. If all religions originate in Chayyah and Yechidah consciousness, are all religions true? My answer: yes and no.

There are two kinds of truth propagated by religion. One is the truth found in its myths and legends, and the rituals these support. The other is the truth of its wisdom teachings and the behaviors these teachings support. There is no way to test the first to establish its truth or its falsehood. The myths, legends, and rituals of a faith must be accepted or rejected on faith, which is why those who do accept them are called the faithful.

There is a way, however, to test the wisdom teachings of a religion, and these teachings should be accepted only if they are proven true. Let me explain.

Begin with myth and legend. Can we prove that Noah built an ark and saved the animals? Did he or his wife or his children leave behind a diary that documents their adventure? No. All we have is the Torah's account. Now for some that is all they need. If Torah says it, it must be true. But this is faith. It cannot be tested.

Imagine a man in our village coming into a court of law with a paper, which he himself wrote, entitling him to one-hundred acres of prime farmland. The judge would inquire into the validity of this paper: "Where did you get this paper?"

Assuming the man to be honest, he would say, "I wrote it myself."

"Then how," the judge would continue, "can we know your claim is true?"

"It is validated by this paper."

"There is no other proof?"

"No. Only this paper. But the paper claims to be true, and I claim it to be true, so it must be true."

The case would be thrown out of court. It is not good enough that the paper justifies itself. There must be objective, outside validation. This is true of the myths of Torah and every other scripture. The truth of the Torah is claimed only in the Torah and those subsequent books based upon it. Torah says it is the true record of God's encounter with the Jews, but its reasoning is circular, and therefore its claim is invalid.

The same is true for the Christian legend that Jesus of Nazareth rose from the dead. Can this be tested? No. One accepts it on faith. It is written in the Gospels and pious Christians accept it the way a pious Jew accepts the Torah. But this is acceptance from faith not proof.

Islam, too, faces the same challenge. The Koran tells us that it is the word of God spoken to Mohammed by the angel Gabriel. How do we know this is true? Because the Koran says it is true. This, again, is circular reasoning and invalid as an objective criterion for proving its claim. It is fine if one chooses to believe this as long as one knows that it cannot be objectively proven.

So what do we do with the myths, legends, and rituals of our particular faith? We hold them out of love, but we hold them with great humility, knowing that we cherish their truth out of faith and that faith can be misplaced.

Things are very different when we look at the wisdom teachings of the different religions.

For example, Torah says that peace comes to those who are just, kind, generous, and honest; who rest on the Sabbath, and curb their desires by keeping kashrut and giving tzedakah. This is not a matter of faith. This is a claim that can be tested. Live the way of Torah and see if the claim is true.

Christians say the same about taking Jesus into your heart. Moslems speak similarly about adhering to the teachings of the Prophet. Test them and see. Not that you have to enter into every religion personally. Look to its followers. If they are kind and loving, their claims that their faith makes them so are true. If they are violent and fearful, the claim that their God brings love is obviously false.

But before you rush to judgment, be careful regarding whom you use as your guide. You remember Berel the Braggart? He was a fool when sober and an ass when drunk. Would you want a Gentile to test the truths of Torah by looking at Berel?

Or take Rav Chalesky. A more bitter and angry man I have yet to meet. His Torah is bitter and his faith is angry; do I want to be judged based on him? Yes, he is knowledgeable, but he is far from wise.

So do not look to bias your judgment by picking an unfair guide. Whom should you pick? I would say the saints and tzaddikim. You want to know if the testable claims of Torah are true? Look to the life of the Baal Shem Tov. You want to know whether the testable claims of Christianity are true? Look to the life of Saint Francis. You want to know the truth of Islam? Look to Rumi. Look to the best toward which we can climb, and not the worst toward which we all too often fall.

Of course, one who then follows a path that is disproved would be a fool. But would any path be disproved? When you pull back the mythic claims of any faith do they not all point to the same virtues? Is there a faith that says "hate your neighbor"? Is there a faith that says God is unjust and values injustice? Is there a faith that does not claim to make its people kinder, more compassionate, more generous?

At this level they all posit the same truths, the same virtues. And these are testable. And they will pass any test: better to be just than unjust, better to be merciful than cruel, better to be generous than stingy.

So, are all religions the same? No when it comes to the myths they believe in. Yes when it comes to the virtues they uphold.

Now we must ask: if the virtues are universal why is there so much violence associated with religion? Because people lack humility when it comes to their myths. They are taught that myths matter most; that God loves only the myth believer, and cannot abide even the virtuous nonbeliever. And why are they taught this? Because the power of the clergy lies not in virtue but in myth.

It is the clergy that compete amongst themselves and with different faiths. The people are just grateful to find a kind soul. Had there been no power associated with becoming the successor to my friend, there would be no infighting among his students. Separate religion from power and it will teach only peace.

I am tired still from my travels, and even thinking about what is being done to Reb Micah's legacy exhausts me. My love to your wife.

B'Shalom

SPIRITUALITY

My dearest Aaron Hershel,

Your business is good, Sarah Leah is with child, and you still have time for me. I am blessed. And I must admit to being flattered by your letter when you wrote that my letters to you were like messages from the prophets. Flattered, but not fooled. And do not allow yourself to be fooled either. I make no claim to prophetic insights. What I think I know of truth is just what I think I know. It is my opinion. It is not *Torah mi Sinai* (divine revelation). If you find our sharing helpful, good. But do not make more of it than it is.

Now, to your questions about spirituality. This is not a Jewish idea, Aaron Hershel. Should I worry that you are becoming too much the American? I am intrigued by the distinction between religion and spirituality, and perhaps I can learn from it. We shall see.

If I understand your letter properly, spirituality is a personal feeling of connectedness to God that arises outside the confines and structures of what you called organized religion. If you imagine that Judaism is organized I suspect you have not been to shul lately. A more disorganized religion I cannot imagine. But I understand what you mean. Do we need religion or can we rely on our inner feeling of connectedness to God?

If we were all prophets and sages, if we were all capable of setting aside the self and opening to the insights and truths of God, then I would say: No, we do not need religion for each of us would tap the One God, the God that is oneness, and know for ourselves what is true. And this knowing would be the same for all of us. Look to our prophets. They lived at different times and in differing circumstances, yet their message is a shared call for justice and compassion. Did they need the organized religion of their day? No.

We need religion because for many of us access to the higher worlds is too difficult to achieve. We need religion to remind us that these higher worlds exist, even if we ourselves cannot reach them. We need religion to point to the truths these higher worlds impart. We need religion to help us put our self-centered lives in a larger context so that we can appreciate the mysteries of birth, love, and death.

Of course, the religion we need is a religion of great humility; a religion that does not lay claim to being the sole embodiment of truth; a religion that can laugh at itself and reform itself and continually realign itself with timeless truth rather than the distortions of truth that happen over time. I suspect that the religion we need is itself in need, and what it needs is this spirituality of which you speak.

So our question is not do we need religion; the question is does religion need spirituality? And the answer is yes. If spirituality, as you defined it for me in your letter, is the higher awareness of Atzilut and Adam Kadmon then spirituality is to religion what sap is to a tree—its lifeblood. Religions should teach people how to move from self-centered Beriah to soul-centered Atzilut and spirit-centered Adam Kadmon. Religions should cultivate prophets and mystics and not run from them. And to do this religions need spirituality.

The question now becomes, how can religions remain open to spirituality? If the nature of religion is to give way to distortion and power disguised as truth and piety, can we expect it to welcome those men and women of the spirit who come to return the faith to the truth? The history of religion is often stained by the blood of its prophets and saints murdered at the hands of its most pious rulers. So what hope is there for religion?

I believe that while it is no doubt difficult, it is still true that religions do reform. I place my hope not in the willingness of the leadership to change, but in the bravery of the people to transform both themselves and their world, and in this way push their religions to realign with the higher truth of one God, one world, one humanity, and one moral code based on universal justice and kindness. I believe that as long as the people continue to struggle for their own connection with God and godliness, as long as you and I commit ourselves to tikkun and teshuvah, there is the opportunity to free religion from the idols of power and fear, and return it to the universal truths of freedom and love.

Another question comes to mind as I think of this: Can there be a spirituality without religion? You spoke of meeting people who claim to be spiritual but not religious. I don't know if this is possible. I am not sure what it means. Sap with no tree to reside in, is this possible? I think that spirituality needs religion to give it a voice.

Let me end with this: There is no living sap without a tree to house it. The tree needs the sap and the sap needs the tree. Indeed, neither can be either without the other. What is true for trees and sap is true for religion and spirituality. They need each other.

B'Shalom

PRAYER

My dearest Aaron Hershel,

I am so glad to hear that Sarah Leah is well and her labor was light. A daughter is a great blessing, and Mashe Mindle is a beautiful name. May she grow in the ways of wisdom, love, and good deeds!

So I should help you think through the idea of prayer. Your questions were clear enough: What is prayer? What is the purpose of prayer? Does God answer prayer? Can prayer change God's mind? As always I am impressed with your thoughts on these matters. Now I will share my own.

What is prayer? Prayer is a conversation between Neshamah and Chayyah, between the self that imagines itself apart from God and the Self that knows itself to be a part of God. The purpose of such a conversation is to till the hard-packed soil of Neshamah and let in the healing and life-giving breath of Chayyah.

How does this tilling happen in prayer? When we pray, we read from our *siddur* (prayer book) the words that have been handed down to us over centuries. These words contain the highest ideals of our people. We read them to remind ourselves of these ideals and to measure the quality of our actions against them. For example, we rise each morning and thank God for our return to wakefulness. We say, "My God, the spirit You breathe into me is pure." If you are praying with *kavvanah,* full attention, you cannot help but ask yourself: How well am I doing with regard to maintaining the purity of this spirit?

This questioning is how you till the soil of Neshamah through prayer. This is also why the verb "to pray," *hitpallel,* is self-referential. It literally means "to observe oneself," and that is what prayer is: self-observation from the moral high ground of Chayyah consciousness.

The result of this prayer is a renewed commitment to these values. And in this renewed commitment we find the answer to our prayer.

Of course, I can hear your objection: "I thought the answer to my prayers was having God do for me what I can't do for myself: heal my family, bring us prosperity and joy." True, this is the conventional notion of the purpose of prayer, but it is not mine.

For so many people God is a cosmic butler whose sole purpose seems to be to fulfill our every desire. This is not my understanding of God. God is what is. To ask God to change the world is to ask God to be other than what God is. And that not even God can do.

So the fact that people pray to God to make things other than they are simply tells us about the nature of Neshamah and nothing about the truth of God. The power of prayer is in reminding Neshamah of the values of Chayyah and its capacity to bring those values to bear in its ordinary dealings in the everyday world. When Neshamah remembers and acts in accordance with these higher values, Neshamah's prayers are answered truly and well.

These are a few thoughts on formal prayer, now let me comment a bit on informal prayer. Informal prayer should be the spontaneous outpouring of the heart. Do not ask for anything; simply thank God for what is and look for guidance in dealing with your shortcomings and problems. This prayer, too, may start out as a conversation. This is natural, for this is how Neshamah communicates: one self talking to another. But if done well and with great kavvanah private prayer moves beyond Neshamah's conversation and becomes a sweet surrender of Neshamah into the unity that is Yechidah.

Let me share with you how this is done. I learned this practice from a student of the sainted rebbe Nachman of Breslov, and while I have adapted it to my own needs, it still retains the core of his practice. He called it *hitbodedut,* secluding oneself in God. Make time each day to be alone. If you can, remove yourself from the business and noise of life and take refuge in the fields or forests. Walk gently until you find a rhythm that allows you to drop all thoughts of your physical self. This allows Nefesh to melt into the background of your awareness. Then look around at the glory of your surroundings. Feel the majesty of creation, and allow Ruach to fill with the beauty of nature.

When you are ready call out to God. Speak out loud. Begin with calling God's Name. Yes, the ultimate Name of God is ineffable, but there are others we can speak. I use *HaRachaman,* the Compassionate One. I call this name aloud over and over and over until I find myself in the presence of God's compassion. My Neshamah is open to the love that is Chayyah and ready to surrender to the emptiness that is Yechidah. I speak to God of all that troubles me. I ask only to be heard; only to be held in the compassionate embrace of Chayyah.

There are days when I talk and talk and talk and not much happens. But there are other days when I talk and then fall silent. It is not a willful silence, not a silence imposed by Neshamah. It is that Neshamah has spoken and been heard and there is nothing more to say. Then there is listening.

We have talked about listening before, and I will not repeat myself. Suffice it to say that when I listen well the "I" that listens disappears and there is, odd as it may seem, only listening. This is the awareness that is Yechidah. There is no "I," only God. And in this there is deep and abiding healing.

There are not words for what I experience in this place of solitude. I know this sounds mysterious and abstract. That is because writing about hitbodedut is so removed from practicing it. In fact, hitbodedut is not mysterious at all.

Here is a good way to understand what is happening. In Hebrew the word for the first person singular is *ani* and, as we have said so many months ago, the word for emptiness is *Ayn.* Ani and

Ayn would appear to be opposites with nothing in common. The ani is our most precious expression of Yesh while Ayn is empty of all form. Yet both words are made up of the same three Hebrew letters: *aleph, yud,* and *nun.* They differ only in the ordering of these letters. When the yud is on the end of the word we have *ani, I.* When the yud is in the middle of the word we have *Ayn,* emptiness.

Our sages saw a great truth in this oddity of the Hebrew language. For them, the yud stands for *yadah,* consciousness. When yadah is focused outside of ourselves we create ourselves—ani, or as we have been speaking of it, Neshamah. When our awareness is focused inside ourselves, when we practice some form of lech lecha, inward turning, we empty ourselves of self and become Ayn. Becoming Ayn is Neshamah opening to Yechidah. Hitbodedut is a way of shifting yadah inward.

When this happens, when ani melts into Ayn and Neshamah surrenders to Yechidah, I understand and experience the wisdom of King David when he sang *kalta nafshi,* ("My soul is obliterated," Psalm 84:30). This is what our kabbalists call *bittul she-me-'ever le-ta'am va-daat* (annihilation beyond reason and knowledge, the end of thought).With the ending of thought comes the ending of ani and Neshamah. And with the ending of Neshamah comes an overwhelming awareness of the truth of Yechidah: the unity of all things in and as God. And with this comes a deep sense of *ahavah,* compassion and love for creation, which is the wisdom of Chayyah. We cannot remain in Yechidah, and it is this deep love from Chayyah that returns us to the world of Yesh, the world of ani, the world of Neshamah.

Don't give up on prayer, Hershele. Use formal prayer to align yourself with the highest values of our people. And make time for hitbodedut and surrender yourself to the One who is All. It for this reason you were born.

B'Shalom

DREAMS

My dearest Aaron Hershel,

I am pleased to hear that you have stopped your traveling. Horses can be a good business, but you are gone too often and for so long. Sarah Leah and Masha Mindle must miss and need you. And now another child is on the way! I will do as you ask and send a bit of red ribbon to protect mother and baby. (A red ribbon was thought to ward off the Evil Eye.)

Do they believe in such things in your America? Here it is commonplace and yet I suspect most do not believe. Either in demons or the power of a red ribbon. But I will send it and I will tell you why. First, because you asked. But secondly, because while I do not believe in demons I do believe in anxiety. Looking at the red ribbon connects us with something higher that we intuitively feel is protective of us. It can allay worry and anxiety, and that can lessen pain. And for that I will send the ribbon. And, yes, I will bless it. It will come to you filled with love.

I had expected your letter would address the topic of hitbodedut and was surprised that instead you want to talk about dreams. You were right to remind me that in my last letter I mentioned that Neshamah opens to Chayyah and Yechidah through prayer, meditation, and dreams. We have spoken of the first two, now let us take up the third.

There are three ways to look at dreams. One, they are the meanderings of a sleeping mind; they mean and signify nothing. Two, they are omens of the future, warnings and signs that reveal what is about to happen; they are meaningful and must be unraveled. Three, that they are a mixture of nonsense and super sense; that is to say, some dreams are or contain the meanderings of a sleeping mind and other dreams or other parts of a dream offer insights from the world of Atzilut breaking through into the world of Beriah. I am interested in dreams from this third perspective.

Dreams are one of the voices of Atzilut; one of the ways the transcendent power of Atzilut is felt in the world of Beriah. There are others: music, art, and poetry, to name a few. But of all the voices of Atzilut, dreaming is the most common. Not everyone can write or paint, play an instrument, or even enjoy fine music. But everyone dreams. And the dream messages that come to us from Atzilut are all the same: "This way lies unity; that way lies separation."

So what is the problem? The problem is that Beriah wants no part of Atzilut. Beriah fears Atzilut because Neshamah imagines that to access Chayyah is a kind of suicide. So Neshamah resists Chayyah; the smaller self seeks to block out the wisdom of the larger self. Neshamah is wrong in its thinking. Tapping into the wisdom and compassion of Chayyah can only enhance the way Neshamah experiences the world around it, but it is difficult to convince Neshamah of this. Nonetheless, there are times when Neshamah cannot resist the presence of Chayyah, and dream sleep is one of these times. In a dream, a meaningful not meandering dream, Chayyah points Neshamah toward wholeness.

When Neshamah is moving toward wholeness on its own, our dreams are affirming, pointing out further steps on our journey. When Neshamah is moving toward separateness our dreams are warning signs, sometimes frightening ones. Chayyah is trying to get Neshamah's attention: "Look where you are going. This is the way of monstrousness and death. Turn around."

As I am writing this I am reminded of a game you used to play as a child. You would close your eyes and your friends would hide a bucket somewhere nearby. Then with your eyes still closed you would search for the bucket. When you moved toward the bucket your friends called out words of encouragement. When you moved away from the bucket they called out words of warning. They only had one goal in mind: helping you find the bucket.

This is a fine analogy for dreams. Chayyah is your friend calling to Neshamah: "Yes, this way; no, not that way." The bucket is the realization of the unity of self and other, Neshamah and Chayyah, Beriah and Atzilut. The bucket is the union of all opposites without negating any of them.

Our dreams tell us when we are moving toward unification and when we are moving away from it. But unlike your friends who shouted their message clearly, Chayyah speaks in symbol and metaphor. You have to interpret what Chayyah says to discover if it is affirming or warning.

How do you do this? You could come home and visit Feige the fortune teller. She will insist that each symbol of a dream has a set meaning. She will tell you what your dream says, and then you can do with it as you will. And, of course, she will charge you. But I would not recommend this.

The dream language of Chayyah is too rich to be reduced to one meaning. If you see a great painting, is there just one way to understand it? If you hear fine music, is there only one way to make sense of it? Of course not, and these, like dreams, come from Atzilut.

There is no one right way to understand a dream. There is only your way. Remember it is your dream, and only you can decide on its meaning. Here is my suggestion: Write your dreams down. Carry them in a journal and mull them over in your mind. Imagine all the possible ways they can be understood and all the possible meanings they may carry. Some will speak to you as being plausible; others will appear absurd. Work with the plausible, but don't dismiss the absurd; they may become plausible over time. Ask yourself: "What might this dream be saying about my life and how I am living it? Is it affirming my path or warning me against it?" Just carry the dream with you and wait. In time you will know the answer. And then you can either heed the dream or ignore it.

What if a dream cannot be understood? What if no answer is ever forthcoming? Let it be. Perhaps it will make sense next month or next year. If a dream is so obscure as to defy understanding, do not break your head over it. Set it aside. Wait for other dreams. They may be clearer, and they may even help you understand the more difficult one.

Enough. It is getting dark and my eyes are growing dim in the darkness. I will sleep soon. And I will dream. And, God willing, I will grow.

B'Shalom

TRUTH

My dearest Aaron Hershel,

No one else asks me such questions! What is truth? I am blessed with you and your questions, I am cursed by trying to invent answers.

I do not know what is truth, if by truth you mean the ultimate secrets of God and universe. I do know a few simple truths, if you want to talk about everyday living. Here is what I know for sure:

It is better for you and others if you are kind, considerate, honest, and just.

It is better for you and others if you judge yourself by your actions rather than your intentions.

It is better for you and others if you learn from your feelings without always acting on them.

It is better for you and others if you are happy—happy people are more generous, forgiving, and helpful.

It is better for you and others if you remember that nothing is permanent.

It is better for you and others if you seek to control yourself rather than them.

It is better for you and others if you say what you mean and do what you say.

It is better for you and others if you value wise silence over learned exposition.

It is better for you and others if you recognize sorrow and joy as natural to life.

It is better for you and others if you see all beings as manifestations of God.

Ten things, that is all I know. They are not mere speculation. Test each one by living it and see if your life is not richer.

I am getting tired earlier and earlier these days. I seem to need more rest and yet get less sleep. Nights are often sleepless for me. Days...their pain is overwhelmed by the wonders of each moment.

B'Shalom

FAITH AND REASON

My Dearest Aaron Hershel,

Now a son to compement your daughter! *Mazal tov!* And a good name you have given him; Chayyim (life). May he be a blessing to all who know him. And then there is the news of your new job—a man with his own store! G'valt! You are becoming a pillar of your community. You make me very proud.

But you write me not only to share news, but to hear my opinions. And today you want to know about the interplay of faith and reason. You know it wasn't so long ago when it was thought that there was no interplay between these two, that they were, in fact, mortal enemies. Thankfully those days are passing, though there are still some who continue the old battle.

For me this issue is not so complicated: I have faith that my reason is reliable, and I find it reasonable to have such faith.

Can you prove to me that you are awake and not dreaming? Are not dreams sometimes so vivid that they are as persuasive as waking? Can you be sure that you are actually reading this letter? Or is it at least a dim possibility that you are asleep and dreaming that you are reading it? But you have faith that when your reason says it is reasonable to assume you are awake, you are in fact awake.

Yet how reliable is faith? Can we test the postulates of faith? Can we find God with a telescope? Among the Christians there is a saying: "I believe because it is absurd." One of their great theologians said this, and when he said it it made perfect sense to him. In other words, he thought it reasonable to believe in the absurd.

Tell me, why do you not believe that Jesus of Nazareth is the only begotten son of God? Thousands upon thousands upon thousands of good, wise, and decent people believe exactly this. And yet you do not. Do you know something they do not know? Or is your belief simply the product of your upbringing?

Thousands upon thousands upon thousands of good, wise, and decent people believe that the Prophet Mohammed, peace be upon him, brought the final revelation from God into the world. And yet Christians do not believe this. Why? Do they know something the Moslems do not? Or is their rejection simply the product of their upbringing?

People believe what they believe because it seems reasonable to them to do so. Why it appears reasonable may have nothing to do with reason and everything to do with faith: they trust the teachings of their parents.

I do not have such trust. I cannot say for certain that Christians are wrong or that the Koran is not God's final holy book. I can only say that given my limited ability to reason these things out, it does not seem reasonable to me that God would impregnate a Jewish woman or limit humanity to a single revelation found in a single book, whether it be Torah or Koran. But I cannot prove any of this. So I must hold my opinion lightly, humbly. I tell you, the people with the deepest faith ought to be the people with the greatest humility. How sad just the opposite proves true.

The Rambam composed what he called the Thirteen Principles of Faith. While never officially accepted and sometimes hotly debated, these principles have over time become the standard statement of Jewish belief. While I do not agree with the Rambam, I find his list helpful in answering your question as to what it is I do believe. So let me list the famous principles of the Rambam and offer the far less famous principles of Yerachmiel ben Yisrael as my own alternatives.

Maimonides: I believe with perfect faith that the Creator, Blessed be His Name, creates and guides all creatures, and that He alone made, makes, and will make everything.

I humbly believe that God is the Source and Substance of all reality.

Maimonides: I believe with perfect faith that the Creator, Blessed be His Name, is unique; there is no uniqueness like His in any way, and that He alone is our God, Who was, Who is, and Who always will be.

I humbly believe that God is one, and that God's oneness necessitates one world, one humanity, and one moral code—justice and compassion for all.

Maimonides: I believe with perfect faith that the Creator, Blessed be His Name, is not physical and is not affected by physical phenomena, and that there is no comparison whatsoever to Him.

I humbly believe that God includes and transcends the physical world; that nature is God manifest in time and space.

Maimonides: I believe with perfect faith that the Creator, Blessed be His Name, is the very first and the very last.

I humbly believe that God is the Ever-Present Reality dwelling in, with, and as all things.

Maimonides: I believe with perfect faith that it is to the Creator, Blessed be His Name, and to Him alone that is it proper to pray and it is not proper to pray to any other.

I humbly believe that God can be understood and approached in many ways, and that no one way is wrong if it leads to universal justice and compassion.

Maimonides: I believe with perfect faith that all the words of the prophets are true.

I humbly believe that the prophets of all nations speak truth when they speak to universal justice and compassion, and false when they do not.

Maimonides: I believe with perfect faith that the prophecy of Moses, our teacher, peace be upon him, was true, and that he was the father of all the prophets—before and after him.

I humbly believe that Moses is among a select group of world teachers who articulate universal truth in a manner suited to their time and historical circumstance.

Maimonides: I believe with perfect faith that the entire Torah now in our hands is the same one that was given to Moses, our teacher, peace be upon him.

I humbly believe that Torah is a historical document reflecting both temporal mores and timeless truths, and that the proper study of Torah sifts through the one to find and affirm the other.

Maimonides: I believe with perfect faith that the Torah will not be exchanged nor will there be another Torah from the Creator, Blessed is His Name.

I humbly believe that revelation is never-ending, and that Torah is one of many sacred texts created by prophets who have opened themselves to God and godliness.

Maimonides: I believe with perfect faith that the Creator, Blessed be His Name, knows all the deeds of human beings and their thoughts.

I humbly believe that our thoughts, words, and deeds can lead us closer to or farther from God and godliness.

Maimonides: I believe with perfect faith that the Creator, Blessed be His Name, rewards with good those who observe His commandments, and punishes those who violate His commandments.

I humbly believe that our thoughts, words, and deeds have consequences and that we must consider them before we speak or act.

Maimonides: I believe with perfect faith in the coming of the Messiah, and even though he may delay, nevertheless I anticipate every day that he will come.

I humbly believe in the future perfection of the world, and understand Judaism at its best to be among the ways to achieve it.

Maimonides: I believe with perfect faith that there will be a resurrection of the dead whenever the wish emanates from the Creator, Blessed is His Name and exalted is His mention, forever and for all eternity.

I humbly believe that I am a temporary manifestation of God, the singular Source and Substance of all reality; that I can glimpse my true nature through meditation and prayer; and that I will fully and joyfully awake to my true nature upon my death.

So, that is what I think. What matters is what you think, for that will determine what you do.

B'Shalom

BE HOLY

My dearest Aaron Hershel,

I will go directly to your question today, for I am already tired and it is not even *Ma'ariv* (evening prayers). You know my father and my zayde, may their memories be for a blessing, lived into their eighties. I suspect I do not have the strength to do likewise. I do not wish to sound maudlin; I am not on my deathbed, but I do want you to know that my love for you has given my life a deeper meaning. For that I am most grateful.

You want to talk about holiness.

Holiness is not some abstract idea. Holiness is the way you and I are to live. This is the meaning behind God's command: "Be holy because I Adonai am holy" (Leviticus 19:2). What a strange demand to make of human beings! We are to be like God. Yet is that not what the serpent said to Eve to entice her to eat of the fruit of the Tree of Knowledge of Good and Evil? (Genesis 3:5) Can it be that the serpent was right all along?

I would say yes, the serpent did know the destiny of humankind. The serpent was the cleverest of all the animals and could discern the potential we humans possess. The mistake the serpent made was twofold. First he was premature. Humanity was not ready to be like God. Adam and Eve had not yet learned what it meant to be humans. To be like God at this point would have meant the Neshamah imagining itself to be God. The all-powerful self is the cause of great suffering, and never holiness.

The second error the serpent made was in equating knowledge with godliness. The serpent says that to eat of the Tree of Knowledge will make you like God. God says that godliness, holiness, is not a matter of knowledge but rather a matter of discovering your true nature.

This is what Torah means when it says we are to "be holy because I, God, am holy." It is because God is holy that we can be holy. The only way such a statement makes sense is if there is a direct connection between God and us. You would not say to a donkey: "Be human because I am human." There is nothing human in the donkey that it could use to comply with your command. So you would never make this demand.

When God commands us to be holy we can imagine one of two things. Either God is speaking nonsense because holiness is beyond humankind, or God is pointing to our innate ability to be godly. If we would not speak nonsense to a donkey, we can assume that God would not speak nonsense to us. And if this is so, then we can also assume that when God says we are to be holy because God is holy, God is pointing to our highest nature and challenging us to live it.

How do we live it? Through the practice of teshuvah, returning our attention over and over again to the present moment and discovering in that moment both the presence of God and the path of godliness. You cannot be holy in the past or future. Holiness is in the now because God is the now. God and godliness manifest together in each moment. To know the first is to do the second. To do the second is to know the first.

Thus Torah teaches: "You shall love the Ineffable God with all your heart" (Deuteronomy 6:5) and "Love your neighbor as yourself" (Leviticus 19:18). I would argue that these are not two different mitzvot but two sides of the same mitzvah. To love God is to discover God present in and as all things. So to love God is to love your neighbor. In loving your neighbor you recognize your connection with your neighbor in the greater unity of God. So to love your neighbor is to love God. The two commandments are simply different ends of the same stick! And the stick itself is love. Where is this love to be lived? In the only place life can be lived, in the present moment. And teshuvah is the practice of returning to the present moment.

When we learn to see God as all in All, we no longer insist upon our absolute separateness, our absolute being, our absolute reality. When we see God as all in All we see everything as empty of absolute being. Our own separateness is surrendered and we are one with all and God.

To be holy, then, is to live the unity of Yesh and Ayn. Living this unity, we know what is right in so powerful a way that we feel commanded to do it. There is no real choice. The knowing is too strong. Neshamah is so open to Chayyah that it can no longer deny the love, justice, and compassion that shape Chayyah's understanding of reality and how to engage it.

Imagine your right hand trying to convince you to cut off your left hand. You would not do it. It is not a choice since cutting off your left hand isn't an option. You do not see your right hand and left hand as separate and competing beings. You know that to harm one would be to harm the whole. This same awareness is present when you practice teshuvah. When you become fully awake in the present moment you see all diversity linked in a greater unity. Harming another living being is a harming of oneself. It isn't a choice.

This choiceless awareness is what our teachers call mitzaveh, being divinely commanded. We are commanded not by a Commander outside of life, but by the commanding sense of unity that is life.

Having said all this, I do not wish to leave you with the impression that there are no guidelines for holiness. Whenever I wish to remind myself of what living a life of holiness is like I turn to the prophet Micah: "What does God require? To do justly, to love mercy, and to walk humbly with your God" (Micah 6:8).

Do justly. To do justly we must know and honor the diversity of Creation. Justice is the establishment of fair and equitable means of interaction between seemingly autonomous beings. Justice is the right running of the world. To do justly we must learn to respect, honor, and preserve the diversity that is the world.

Love mercy. To love mercy is to be motivated by compassion. Compassion arises from a sense of shared suffering. Shared suffering arises from our awakening to the oneness that underlies our diversity. We love mercy and act with compassion to the extent we identify with others. Perceiving the unity of self and other immediately translates into ahavah for both self and other.

Walk humbly with God. This means to walk lightly and not take yourself too seriously. You cannot walk with God and self at the same time. The self can maintain itself only by insisting it is separate from God and the whole. Walking humbly means to stop insisting you are more than you are.

But do not imagine a humble self is a weak self. On the contrary, a humble self is a powerful self for it is grounded in all of life and filled with the spirit of the Source of life. It is just not a foolish self. A foolish self insists it is alone, and that it must defend itself against all other selves. A humble self knows there is no aloneness in the world, only connectedness. A humble self knows the truth of Hillel's saying "If I am not for myself who will be for me, and if I am only for myself, what am I?" (Pirke Avot 1:14). A humble self honors itself and others for it sees itself as one with others.

So, what am I saying with all these words? Being holy means making teshuvah and thus being present to each moment. Being present reveals your connection with all life, and calls forth justice and compassion. Doing justly and compassionately is loving your neighbor. Loving your neighbor is loving God. Loving God is loving it all.

B'Shalom

JESUS

My dearest Aaron Hershel,

You wrote me once about how America is different, that in America a person is free to follow whatever religion he or she chooses. And yet now you tell me how very Christian a place America is. So? Is this supposed to be news to me? Did I think that America was a nation of Jews? No. You and I both knew that when you left home for America you were leaving behind the security of a Jewish village. But you have done well in America, and our continued correspondence tells me that we did not lose a Jew when you left home.

But you cannot escape Jesus, and want to know what I think of him. You know most rabbis would not respond to your question. You want to know what I think of Jesus? To even have an opinion is to put me at the fringe of our faith. Unless of course that opinion is that Jesus is a figment of the Christian imagination.

But to be honest, I am not disinterested in this man Jesus. How can we ignore one who inspires millions? How can we ignore the most famous Jew in all the world?

There are so many opinions about him. There are those who say he is the Son of God. There are those who say he is the illegitimate son of a Jewish woman whose messianic claims were simply an attempt to have God take the place of his missing father. Others say he was a prophet, a rabbi, or a revolutionary fighting Rome.

My own opinion is this: He was a great soul whose Neshamah was open to the highest levels of Yechidah. Those who read the words of Jesus assume that he was talking about himself as a Neshamah; that when he said "I and the Father are one" he was referring to himself in the same way he might say, "I am going to the market."

I do not believe this. The "I" that goes to the market is Neshamah. The "I" that is one with God is Yechidah. Jesus is not speaking from the perspective of Beriah, but to Beriah from the perspective of Adam Kadmon. All of his sayings should be read as an attempt to articulate the absolute unity of all things in, with, and as God. And almost every prophet that has revealed this truth has died at the hands of those it threatened most.

In Jesus's case these are the Romans and those Jews who collaborated with them. The Jewish establishment had built for itself a world based on clear divisions: Jew and Gentile, clean and unclean, holy and unholy, permitted and forbidden. But these divisions make sense only from the perspective of Beriah. They do not exist in Adam Kadmon. Yechidah consciousness does not see the chosen and the rest; Yechidah sees only God. Jesus speaking from Yechidah threatened their entire system.

The Romans wanted only capitulation on the part of those nations it occupied. Pay your taxes and do not challenge the supremacy of Rome or the divinity of the Caesar and you will be allowed to live. But if you threaten the status quo in any way you will be mercilessly crucified. Jesus drew crowds. Jesus spoke of another kingdom, the kingdom of God not Caesar. Jesus was a threat and had to die.

So it is no surprise that the Romans crucified Jesus. Did he rise from the dead on the third day after his burial? This is one of the unprovable myths that the faithful should hold with deep humility. I do not believe he did, but I can no more prove my opinion than the pope in Rome can prove his.

Is Jesus a traitor to the Jews? I do not think so. What was his message? When asked to articulate the core mitzvot of Judaism he said: Love God and love your neighbor. Is there anything more Jewish than this? Jesus spoke to and within his people and their culture. He wanted to infuse Judaism with the insights of Yechidah, and in so doing broke many of the taboos the priests and rabbis had set in place. But his actions were no different than the actions of other prophets. They too made radical claims and dramatized their teachings with actions that outraged their contemporaries.

So, I do not find Jesus a problem. Christianity, of course, was not the religion of Jesus. Judaism was the religion of Jesus. Christianity is the religion about Jesus as Christ, the only one through whom we humans can return to God. If Jesus's teaching of love God and love your neighbor is the heart of Judaism, the idea that one needs an intermediary between you and God is the polar opposite from Judaism.

We have spoken of this before. Teshuvah, the capacity to return to God and godliness at any moment leaves no room for a savior. Christians often wonder why we Jews have never accepted their faith. It is because we do not need their faith; it does nothing for us. Christianity solves a problem that we Jews do not have.

Christianity solves the problem of how to bridge the gap between the sinful person and a sinless God. Judaism does not posit this gap. God is never far from us. All we have to do is return to our true nature and God is here.

What more can I say of this? I am not sure what good my opinion will do you, or why it is even of interest. But, since we are talking about prophets let me add something else.

Could it be that Jesus was more open to Yechidah consciousness than most of his contemporaries? Yes. I believe he was. But he is one of many such people throughout time and across every culture. There are always those who are more open to Yechidah than the rest of us, and we need them to remind us that we are more than the separate self Neshamah reveals. But do not imagine that these people are different from you. You have the same capacity to see the world from the perspective of Yechidah.

Think of it this way. Imagine two beautiful women, identical twins, each covered in dozens of veils so that the beauty of both is concealed. Now imagine that one of the sisters begins to remove her veils. At first a few veils makes no difference, she is still impossible to see. But in time she has removed enough of the veils so that the outlines of her face can be seen. She is indeed beautiful. A few more veils and her beauty shines through more clearly. Eventually she will have so few veils left that there is no hiding her glory.

All this time her twin has stood next to her with her veils in place. As you look at the two sisters you cannot help but say the one with the fewest veils is the more beautiful of the two. Yet they are identical twins! They have an equal beauty, but one's beauty is more apparent than the other.

Now think in terms of people. We are all filled with all five dimensions of consciousness. It is not that some of us have more of God than others. We are all manifestations of God. But some of us have worked to remove more of the veils of Neshamah that keep the glory of God hidden from the everyday world. These are people committed to the inward walking, to contemplative prayer, to isolation in God, and in them the divine shines through more clearly. These people seem more connected to God, but in fact they are only more adept at revealing the connection that each of us enjoys.

Jesus was simply a sage who devoted his life to removing the veils and living from the highest perspective of which we humans are capable. We should look to him as a guide not as a god. Christianity points to Jesus, but Jesus points to God. The former I cannot follow, but the latter is a spiritual friend of great value.

I have gone on far longer than I intended. I am very tired.

B'Shalom

FINDING A TEACHER

My dearest Aaron Hershel,

It seems I do not know myself as well as I pretend. What I thought was a temporary illness is not so temporary after all. I thought that I was still in the middle of my days but I discover that I am coming to the end. I am dying. From what, I do not know. Does it matter? Not to me. I am grateful for the time I have had, and grateful too that this dying is slow enough to allow me to settle my affairs. My only prayer now is that I may be conscious as I die, and not lost in delirium.

You know that I believe death to be the opening of Yesh to Ayn and Beriah to Atzilut and then Adam Kadmon. All these are ways of saying that the wave returns to the ocean, I return to God. Death is the ultimate act of teshuvah, and is accompanied by a joy so intense that it eliminates even the self that enjoys it. It is pure bliss, pure spirit without a self or soul to get in the way of the absolute unity of God. I want to be awake for the birth of this joy. I want to give thanks as I glimpse the total oneness of all things. I want to recite the Sh'ma and affirm the absolute unity of all things in God as I melt for the last time into that Unity Itself.

But this is not mine to decide. I will have to accept whatever is offered.

I tell you all this to inform you of my situation, to alleviate any fear or worry you may have for me, and as an excuse for not responding to the question you raised in your last letter. While my mind is yet clear, I do not have the strength for questions. No, that is not exactly it. It is more that I find it less and less necessary to ask and to answer.

The knowing is becoming so clear that I realize my words can only confuse. So I beg your forgiveness if I put your questions aside.

But I do not want your questioning to end just because I am no longer here to answer. It is time to find another teacher. Some wonderful rabbis have made America their home. Seek them out. And do not think you can learn only from your own. There are sages of every tradition who can enlarge your mind and broaden your perspective. Do not limit yourself by labels.

I will not suggest anyone in particular. I do not know any that well. But I want to tell you what to look for. There are four qualities in a true teacher: humility, patience, wisdom, and the ability to speak to you where you are so that you may go where the teacher has gone.

Humility is the recognition that the teacher is not the teaching. The perfect message does not imply a perfect messenger. Teachers should respect their humanness and control their behavior, treating all beings with respect. They should respect their limitations and recognize the truth flowing from other streams of which they may be ignorant. They should respect their students, seeking to teach them and not exploit them.

Patience is the ability to allow a student to ripen in his or her own time. (Yes, her! Did you think I would rob Mashe Mindle of her right to know the truth of who she is?) There are some who learn quickly and some who learn slowly. The teacher must honor the student's nature. Patience also means the willingness to listen to student's questions and answer them for the benefit of the student and not to prove the teacher's superiority.

Wisdom is the quality of the teacher's teachings. If what is taught is irrational, do not accept it. If a teacher teaches that which makes no sense, do not assume it is you who are senseless. Teachers teach what they know, and some may know very little, inventing the rest for their own self-aggrandizement. Listen to your heart, and do not engage in actions that are harmful or disrespectful. Listen to your head, and do not bother with teachings that are inconsistent, contradictory, or without reason. The teacher's teachings must be in line with the principle of l'chayyim. They must move you toward wholeness and holiness. They must root your words and deeds in respect for all life as a manifestation of God.

The ability to reach a student is crucial. Teachers may be very wise, but if they cannot transmit their wisdom it is of no use to anyone but themselves. Teachers must have the skill to know when students need answers and when it is better to just let them be with their questions. Teachers must know when to push and when to pull, when to comfort and when to confront, when to hold on and when to let go.

I am sorry, Aaron Hershel, there was more I wanted to say but I cannot remember it. I am again growing tired. Just remember this: The truth cannot be possessed by teachers or by traditions. If a teacher points beyond self and tradition to something shared by all, then look to see where the pointing is aimed. If a teacher points only to self or tradition, look for another teacher.

B'Shalom

DEATH

My dearest Aaron Hershel,

Our sages say that a parent is one who raises a child, not simply creates one. Have I had the honor of raising you a bit? I allow myself the conceit of thinking so.

It has been quite some time since I last wrote you. Your letters have arrived and were read to me, for my eyes no longer see. I have not responded because I am too weak to write and my thoughts not clear enough to dictate to another. But now I have no choice.

This letter is being written for me by my dear friend, Chayyim Beryl. I suspect that by the time this letter reaches you I will be gone. The stream of life that was me is now poured out into the sea of life that is God. Do you think God will know me? Challenge me to prove I am worthy of heaven?

I do not think this is so. The flow of the stream is not concerned with the foam on its surface. Knowing and challenging are for the living, not for Life. Life is all-welcoming, all-accepting. We create heaven and hell here on earth, the only place such things matter. With God there is only peace.

Heaven and hell are fantasies of the Neshamah, the seemingly separate self. It is the Neshamah's last attempt to impose its will on reality. The closer I come to death the weaker my Neshamah's ability to insist upon its own immortality and impose its own will. The closer I come to death the more Neshamah opens to Chayyah, and realizes it is not apart from the Whole but a part of the Whole. With the awakening to Chayyah, Yesh and Ayn are seen as one, and this seeing floods me with joy. The fear of death that is the hallmark of Neshamah surrenders to the peace and joy of Chayyah. And if Chayyah is joy, Yechidah, my complete return to God is pure bliss; a bliss so limitless and overwhelming that it swallows me up like a drop of water returning to the sea. I become what I always am.

Reb Aaron, this is Chayyim Beryl. Reb Yerachmiel is sleeping. We will continue when he awakes. We are all so sad about his passing. Even those who disagreed with him visit to honor him. He was a simple soul filled with much wisdom. We send our best to you and your family in this time of grief.

My dear Aaron Hershel, Reb Chayyim tells me I dozed off. I have certainly lost my train of thought and cannot bear to review what I have had him write to you. I suspect that if Reb Chayyim expects me to awake from my next nap, he will be very disappointed.

I ask your forgiveness for not continuing our conversation. I write now only to say goodbye and to thank you for your love. There is nothing a rabbi cherishes more than a student who trusts enough to question.

Listen, my sweet Aaron Hershel, death is real in this world of Yesh. Do not deny it. Do not cover it over with dreams of eternity, afterlife, or rebirth. All this is a denial of death's simple reality: When we look at the world from the perspective of Yesh, we see birth and we see death. When we look at the world from the perspective of Ayn, we see no birth and no death. Both are true. Yesh and Ayn are poles of a Greater Unity: Only God is real, for only God is whole and complete.

Yes, Reb Yerachmiel ben Yisrael is gone, but the One who wore his face for these many years is ever present. And that One wears your face as well. What we truly are is God manifest in time and place. Know this and live well until you die.

You have been a blessing to me beyond anything words can convey. Remember, "love is stronger than death" (Song of Songs 8:6). Shortly I will be no more. Let our love grow ever stronger.

B'Shalom

Reb Aaron,

This is Chayyim Beryl. Reb Yerachmiel has died. He passed in his sleep early this morning. He knew it was coming and gathered his students around him. I was asked to stay as well. He looked at each one as if he could see through them. To each he smiled and nodded. His last words were these: "The essence of God is that there is no essence of God, for God is all and nothing here, now, and forever." His eyes closed and then he fell asleep. He did not awake. Or, then again, perhaps he did.

GLOSSARY

Adam	earthling
Adam Kadmon	Literally "primordial being," the dimension of life corresponding to the nonduality of all things as God.
adamah	earth
Adonai	Lord. A euphemism for the ineffable Name of God derived from the Hebrew verb "to be."
ahavah	love
aleph	The first letter of the Hebrew alphabet.
ani	I
Assiyah	Literally "action," the dimension of life corresponding to the laws of nature.
Atzilut	Literally "emanation," the dimension of life corresponding to the unity and interdependence of all things in God.
Aveinu	Our Father
avodah be-bittu	Literally, "the work of annihilation," meditative emptying of self into the nonduality of God.
Ayn	Emptiness
Beit Midrash	House of Study
Bereshit	Genesis, the first of the Five Books of Moses.
Beriah	Literally "creation," corresponding to the dimension of life that supports self-aware beings.
Besht	An acronym for the Baal Shem Tov.
bittul she-me-'ever le-ta'am va-data	Annihilation beyond reason and knowledge, the end of thought.
bris	ritual circumcision
B'Shalom	In peace
chamesh	Five
chametz	Leavened foods to be avoided during Passover.
Chayyah	Literally "living thing," corresponding to the fourth level of consciousness where all beings are seen as interconnected and part of the one Being, God.
chayyim	life
cheshbon hanefesh	Accounting of the soul, a daily review of one's life assessing the quality of ones actions against the ideals of the thirteen Attributes of God.
Chumash	five Books of Moses
chuppah	wedding canopy
drash	Metaphorical reading of text.
Ehyeh Asher Ehyeh	The Name of God revealed to Moses at the Burning Bush.

	Conventionally translated "I am what I am," it is more accurately understood as "I am all that was, is, and will be."
eishet chayil	A woman of valor
El	God
Elohut	Godhead
Gan Eden	Garden of Eden
Gemorah	The book of law and ethics that, together with the *Mishnah,* make up the Talmud, the code book of Jewish living.
gerushin	contemplative repetition of a sacred phrase or Name of God.
g'valt	expression of shock or sorrow
Haggadah	Passover prayer book
Halachah	Jewish law
Hanukkah	Festival of Light
HaRachaman	The Compassionate One
HaShem	Literally "the Name" but used to refer to the ineffable Name of God.
hitbodedut	Secluding oneself in God.
hitpallel	To pray
Kalta nafshi	"My soul is obliterated" (Psalm 84:30]
kashrut	Jewish dietary laws
kavvanah	full attention
ketubah	wedding contract
Ketuvim	Literally "Writings," referring to the third section of the Hebrew Bible including Psalms, Proverbs, Ecclesiastes, etc.
ki tov	Good, worthwhile; God's assessment of creation.
klippot	shells
l'chayyim	"To life," the guiding principle behind all Jewish spiritual practices.
Lech lecha	"walk inward," referring to those Jewish spiritual practices that strip away one's conditioning.
lishma	Something done for its own sake.
loshen hora	Literally "hurtful speech" but used as shorthand for "avoiding hurtful speech" or for compassionate speech.
Ma'ariv	Evening prayers
Mashiach	Messiah
mazal tov	congratulations
mensch	A good, kind, and just person.
Menschlichkeit	The way of being good, kind, and just; the way of godliness.
meshugas	craziness
mezzuzah	Box containing the Sh'ma attached to doorposts.

minyan	Prayer quorum of ten people.
Mishnah	The book of law and ethics that, together with the *Gemorah*, make up the Talmud, the book of Jewish living.
mitzvah/ mitzvot	Commandment/s or religious obligation/s.
mitzaveh	command
Mitzrahim	Egypt, "the narrow places"
nachas	pride, joy
nefesh	Literally "breath," refers to the level of consciousness found in the autonomic nervous system.
Neshamah	Literally "breath," refers to the egoic or self-aware level of consciousness.
Nevi'im	Prophets
nun	The Hebrew letter "n."
olam	world
or l'goyyim	Light unto the nations.
Pesach	Passover
Pirke Avot	*The Sayings of the Fathers*, an ancient anthology of rabbinic teachings
pshat	Literally "simple" referring to the surface reading of a text.
Rabbeinu	Our Teacher
Rambam	Acronym for Rabbi Mosen ben Maimon, also known as Maimonides (10th century).
remez	Literally "hint," referring to the allegorical reading of text.
Ribbono shel Olam	Teacher of All Worlds
Rosh haShanah	Jewish New Year
Ruach	Literally "wind," refers to the instinctual level of consciousness.
Sh'ma	Literally "Listen!" refers to the central affirmation of Judaism: "Listen, O Israel, the Ineffable Reality is our God. The Ineffable is One."
Shabbat	Sabbath
shanda	scandal
Shavuot	Feast of Weeks celebrating the giving of the Ten Commandments on Mount Sinai.
shivah	Seven day mourning period.
Shlemut	Divine wholeness, completeness, nonduality.
shul	synagogue
siddur	Hebrew prayer book
Sod	Literally "secret," referring to the mystical reading of text
Sukkot	Literally "booths," the structures used to store the harvest, refers to the fall Harvest Festival.

tallit	prayer shawl
Tanakh	Acronym for the Hebrew Bible: *Torah* (the Five Books of Moses), *Nivi'im* (Prophets), and *Ketuvim* (Writings).
tefillah	prayer
tefillin	phylacteries
teshuvah	Literally "return," referring to one's returning attention to the present and rediscovering one's true nature as a manifestation of God.
tikkun	Literally "repair," refers to the practice of engaging all beings with compassion, justice, and respect.
tikkun hanefesh	Literally "repairing the soul," refers to the practice of engaging oneself in a manner that honors and reveals one's connectedness to God.
tikkun haolam	Literally "repairing the world," refers to the practice of engaging others in a manner that honors and reveals their unity with all things in God.
Torah	Five Books of Moses, also used to refer to the totality of Jewish wisdom teaching.
Torah mi Sinai	Torah from Sinai, divine revelation.
treif	Not kosher, heretical.
tzaddik/tzaddikim	Literally "righteous one/s," and often used to refer to spiritual masters in the hasidic tradition.
tzedakah	Literally "justice," refers to acts of financial charity and generosity.
V'ahavta	"And you shall love," the opening line of the prayer that follows the Sh'ma.
yadah	Knowing, awareness, consciousness.
Yechidah	Literally "unity," refers to that level of consciousness where all things are seen as the One Thing, God.
Yesh	Literally "to exist," refers to the world of seemingly separate forms.
yeshivah	School of Jewish learning.
Yetzer haRah	capacity for evil
Yetzer haTov	capacity for good
Yetzirah	Literally "formation," the dimension of life corresponding to instinctual behaviors such as the fight or flight response
yiddishkeit	Jewishness
Yisrael	Israel
Yom Kippur	Day of Atonement
Yontif (Yiddish)	Holy Days
yud	The Hebrew letter "y."
zayde	grandfather

9 780974 935928